CAPM®

Certified Associate in Project Management Practice Exams

James L. Haner, Cate McCoy

New York   Chicago   San Francisco
Athens   London   Madrid   Mexico City
Milan   New Delhi   Singapore   Sydney   Toronto

1 2 3 4 5 6 7 8 9   QVS   21 20 19 18

ISBN   978-1-260-44048-5
MHID   1-260-44048-6

Sponsoring Editor Wendy Rinaldi	**Technical Editor** Warren Soong	**Composition** Cenveo Publisher Services
Editorial Supervisor Patty Mon	**Copy Editor** Lisa McCoy	**Illustration** Cenveo Publisher Services
Project Manager Tuhina Jha, Cenveo® Publisher Services	**Proofreader** Claire Splan	**Art Director, Cover** Jeff Weeks
Acquisitions Coordinator Claire Yee	**Production Supervisor** Lynn M. Messina	

CAPM®

Certified Associate in Project Management Practice Exams

ABOUT THE AUTHORS

James L. Haner, PMP, CAPM, PgMP, PMI-ACP, PMI-RMP, PMI-SP, is the head of Ultimate Business Resources Consulting, specializing in "Building Better Businesses." James's management and leadership roles have included establishing a corporate web presence, creating a successful organization-wide employee development plan, and developing the IT infrastructure for a start-up company.

James brings more than three decades of dynamic experience as a distinguished college professor; award-winning author of books, articles, and blogs; and successful management and leadership consultant to each learning experience.

He is a member of the Project Management Institute (PMI) and the American Society for Training & Development (ASTD). James has won the Dale Carnegie Course "Highest Achievement Award." He earned the Vietnam Service Medal while serving in the U.S. Air Force.

Cate McCoy, PMP, CAPM, PBA, CBAP, is the founding partner of Communi-cate, Inc., a technology management consulting and training company focused on government and corporate clients. She has been immersed in information technology projects for almost 30 years, including technical roles, project management roles, and business analysis roles. Her firsthand experience covers many industries, including government agencies, insurance, banking, and manufacturing. Ms. McCoy earned her master's degree in information systems and her bachelor's degree in computer science from Marist College, Poughkeepsie, New York, while working as a technology professional at IBM in the 1980s. The technical background serves as a solid foundation for the projects she manages and the business analysis insights she brings to projects providing both process-oriented and logic-based insights.

Staying true to her love for writing, Cate serves as author, curriculum advisor, and seminar leader for international training companies, including Learning Tree International. Ms. McCoy is the author and technical editor of several books on technology and management topics and is the curriculum designer and author of over 100 courses on technical, project management, and business analysis.

About the Technical Editor

Warren Soong, PMP, CISSP, is an experienced executive with technical/business leadership and project/program management in technology, finance, and defense industries. After beginning as a network, operating system, and security technician, he advanced through engineer, architect, and management roles. He remains an entrepreneur who has founded, grown, and run multiple diverse, global businesses. Currently he serves as a program director in the systems engineering and cybersecurity fields.

Mr. Soong retired as a U.S. Marine Corps colonel after a distinguished 30-year career on active duty and as a reservist. He earned a master's of science in information technology from the Naval Postgraduate School, Monterey, California, and a bachelor's of arts from Cornell University, Ithaca, New York. In addition to being an educator, he is an author, curriculum developer, and event facilitator for development programs in project and business management, systems engineering, network technologies, MCSE, and CISSP for various organizations and corporations, including several U.S. federal agencies, global financial firms, and leading technology firms.

This book is dedicated to Anna Mae Moss. Yo' Mom, I did it . . . again!

—James

I dedicate this book to my husband,
Tom, who simply refuses to give in to any of my
project management attempts on the home front.
God bless Tom for keeping our relationship in perspective.

—Cate

CONTENTS

ACKNOWLEDGMENTS

The authors wish to acknowledge the McGraw-Hill Education team for their guidance in bringing this book to life. Whether you corrected a typo, added words that clarified our meaning, or pushed an approval through, we know a book is not written by the subject matter experts alone but instead is the product created by a great team.

INTRODUCTION

What Is the CAPM® Certification?

The Certified Associate in Project Management (CAPM) is an entry-level certificate in project management that proves the certificate holder has a solid foundation in project management fundamentals.

Is the CAPM Certification Right for You?

Are you managing projects but don't have the project manager title? Are you a new project manager? Are you working towards becoming a project manager?

If so, you need the knowledge of a project manager but may not yet have acquired the work experience required to achieve the Project Management Professional (PMP) certification. The CAPM certification can be a stepping stone to gaining that work experience.

As a CAPM-credentialed project manager, you have proven that you have the personal motivation needed to distinguish yourself in today's job market. Both the CAPM exam and the PMP exam are based on *A Guide to the Project Management Body of Knowledge (PMBOK Guide), Sixth Edition*. The foundation knowledge is the same!

CAPM PMI Eligibility Requirements

To sit the CAPM exam, the PMI prerequisites are to either have 23 contact hours of project management education or 1,500 hours of project experience (using a 40-hour week as an example, this would be 38 weeks or 8.5 months working on a project team). In addition, a high school diploma or global equivalent is required.

The 1,500 hours of project experience mean that even if you have not directed and led projects (the threshold for the PMP credential) at this point in your career, your project experience is directly applicable to the CAPM credential.

If you choose project management education as your evidence of eligibility, one classroom hour of instruction equals one contact hour (23 are needed). Course content can include project topics such as quality, scope, time, cost, resources, communication, risk, procurement, and integration. Excluded from the 23 contact hours are PMI chapter meetings and any self-directed learning such as reading project management books or watching project management videos.

Typical Job Titles and Roles

CAPM candidates typically have job titles like Project Team Lead, Associate Project Coordinator, Project Analyst, Project Coordinator, and Project Staff Lead. Job roles matter as well, and any role that requires you to manage yourself and others to achieve project goals and create deliverables can benefit from the knowledge required to earn the CAPM certification.

Applying for the CAPM Certification

To apply for the CAPM certification, use a web browser to navigate to https://certification.pmi.org/default.aspx, where you can log in to your existing PMI account or register for a new account. The Certification Program overview page lists your current certifications and certifications for which you are eligible to apply. Click the link to "Apply for the CAPM Credential," confirm your address and contact information, then input the information for the education level you have attained followed by your professional project experience or your project management education hours.

For any questions unique to your situation (e.g., special accommodations), e-mail your question to customercare@pmi.org.

Preparing for the CAPM Exam

To prepare for the exam, read *A Guide to the Project Management Body of Knowledge (PMBOK Guide), Sixth Edition* and drill on practice exam questions like the ones in this book and in the companion Total Tester tool. The CAPM exam is a three-hour timed exam containing 150 multiple choice questions. Each question has four possible answers, and you must choose the single best answer.

Exam Content Outline (ECO)

The 150 questions cover 13 topics in percentages balanced according to the PMI CAPM Exam Content Outline dated May 2018 (commonly referred to as the 2018 ECO). Both the chapters in this book and the companion Total Tester questions are balanced with the ECO.

Chapter Titles	ECO%	300 Chapter Questions	600 Total Tester Questions
Introduction to Project Management	6%	18	36
Project Environment	6%	18	36
Role of the Project Manager	7%	21	42
Project Integration Management	9%	27	54
Project Scope Management	9%	27	54
Project Schedule Management	9%	27	54
Project Cost Management	8%	24	48
Project Quality Management	7%	21	42
Project Resource Management	8%	24	48
Project Communication Management	10%	30	60
Project Risk Management	8%	24	48
Project Procurement Management	4%	12	24
Project Stakeholder Management	9%	27	54

Types of Questions

Many of the questions will test how well you have read and absorbed the information presented in *A Guide to the Project Management Body of Knowledge (PMBOK Guide), Sixth Edition*. You'll be tested at the knowledge, comprehension, and application levels. You can expect questions that ask

- *What is...*
- *Which of...*
- *What are...*
- *What next...*

Inputs, tools, techniques, and outputs are tested. These are commonly referred to as the ITTOs. Each of the processes in *A Guide to the Project Management Body of Knowledge (PMBOK Guide), Sixth Edition* begins with a diagram that defines the ITTO for that process. Questions on ITTOs may be asked, such as "Which of the following is an input to..." and "What would you do next if you have (this set of inputs)...." When asked what to do next, the question will provide you with a short scenario to place you in the context of a real project situation, and based on what project management task you are performing, what inputs you have, and what outputs are created, you will need to distinguish what to do next by choosing the best answer.

The CAPM Exam Experience

The CAPM exam is offered through an online proctored environment taken from your home or work computer, or it can be taken at one of the Pearson VUE testing centers located around the world.

If you are taking the online proctored exam, log in to the exam website 15 to 30 minutes prior to your exam start time. This will give the live web-based proctor a chance to compare your picture identification (license, passport, etc.) with your face and to scan your office with your webcam to make sure your desk is empty (no extra computers, no papers, no books, no anything!). You'll need to pick up your laptop with its embedded webcam or your external webcam and do a 360-degree turn to let the proctor scan your room, then your ceiling, and then your floor. You may not take a break from the test. If you step away from your testing environment before completing your exam, the exam is terminated.

If you are taking the exam at a Pearson VUE testing center, arrive at the testing center 15 minutes prior to your scheduled appointment time. You will be assigned a locker to store your personal items and then escorted into the testing room and assigned a computer cubicle to take your exam. If you step away from your testing environment before completing your exam, the exam clock will continue to count down but does not terminate your exam.

About This Book

This book and its companion Total Tester is a compilation of 900 sample test questions useful to candidates studying to pass the CAPM exam.

In Every Chapter

Each chapter opens with a short narrative describing the purpose of the process group under discussion followed by the bulleted certification learning objectives for the process group. The four to six certification learning objectives for each process group are from the PMI CAPM Exam Content Outline dated May 2018. Each chapter concludes with a set of questions for the process group tied to the certification learning objectives.

In the Total Tester

Included with this book is access to the Total Tester, an online exam engine that contains even more practice questions with detailed explanations of the answers. Using this set of practice questions provided in the Total Tester exam engine is another tool to help you prepare for the CAPM exam. Please see the appendix for more information about accessing the Total Tester.

Introduction to Project Management

In this chapter, you will
- Understand the five project management process groups and the processes within each group
- Recognize the relationships among project, program, portfolio, and operational management
- Define a typical project lifecycle
- Understand the function and importance of tailoring for different projects

The first chapter of *A Guide to the Project Management Body of Knowledge (PMBOK Guide)* sets the stage with important key terms in project management, together with the reasoning behind why project management is valuable to organizations. Certified Associate in Project Management (CAPM) candidates are tested on four objectives that emphasize the need to know the *PMBOK Guide* process names, the relationship of projects to larger initiatives, lifecycles present within projects, and tailoring considerations for the *PMBOK Guide* processes.

The 18 practice questions in this chapter are mapped to the style and frequency of question types you will see on the CAPM exam.

1. Which knowledge area guides a project team in completing work that has been agreed upon with the project sponsor?

    A. Project Quality Management

    B. Project Change Management

    C. Project Scope Management

    D. Project Configuration Management

2. In which process group does the project manager obtain, manage, and use resources to accomplish the project objectives?

    A. Initiating

    B. Executing

    C. Planning

    D. Monitoring and Controlling

3. Which of the following is true of program and portfolio management?

    A. A project manager manages programs, portfolios, and projects.

    B. The objectives of programs, portfolios, and projects are the same.

    C. Programs, portfolios, and projects may share the same lifecycles.

    D. Stakeholders and resources may be the same in programs, portfolios, and projects.

4. What is one of the goals of portfolio management?

    A. Minimize expenses across programs

    B. Manage multiple simultaneous projects

    C. Maximize profit between projects

    D. Mitigate the risks of stand-alone projects

5. The series of phases that a project passes through to create a product is best described as:

    A. Product life cycle

    B. Project life cycle

    C. Program life cycle

    D. Portfolio life cycle

6. Which process groups ensure that the project work is carried out?

    A. Planning and Executing

    B. Initiating and Closing

    C. Executing and Monitoring and Controlling

    D. Monitoring and Controlling

7. Which of the following best describes a system of practices, techniques, procedures, and rules used by those who work in a particular discipline?

   A. Program

   B. Management

   C. Project

   D. Methodology

8. Which of the following competing factors should be the focus of tailoring the project management phases in the PMBOK Guide for individual projects?

   A. Scope, schedule, cost, resources, quality, and risk

   B. Initiating and planning

   C. Risk management and procurement approaches

   D. Teams, managers, matrix, hierarchies, vendors, and collaboration

9. Which stakeholders make the tailoring decision for a project?

   A. Project manager and project sponsor

   B. Project sponsor and organizational management

   C. Project manager and business analyst

   D. The project team

10. Which of the following activities would you undertake as a project manager to best understand the project environment?

    A. Schedule all resources

    B. Identify cultural and social issues

    C. Project budget approval process

    D. Detailed requirements analysis

11. What is the function of the project management office?

    A. Provide standard forms for project paperwork.

    B. Close project accounts at the end of the projects.

    C. Coordinate the management of projects.

    D. Provide hot-desk facilities for all project managers.

12. What is the process called that defines and controls what is and is not included in a given project?

    A. Project Documentation Management

    B. Project Change Control

    C. Plan Scope Management

    D. Governance

13. In which process does a project team work together to define procedures by which the project scope and product scope can be modified?

   A. Validate Scope

   B. Plan Configuration Management

   C. Initial Scope Definition

   D. Control Scope

14. In which knowledge area does the project manager identify the activities, dependencies, and resources needed to produce the project deliverables?

   A. Project Schedule Control Management

   B. Project Risk Management

   C. Project Schedule Management

   D. Project Cost Planning Management

15. Determining the cost of the resources needed to complete the planned schedule of activities on a project is called

   A. Project Risk Management

   B. Project Schedule Management

   C. Project Cost Management

   D. Project Resource Management

16. Which of the following describes the work of monitoring and recording the results of executing quality activities to assess performance and recommend necessary changes?

   A. Control Quality

   B. Perform Quality Assurance

   C. Plan Quality

   D. Quality Improvement

17. The set of project management activities that includes identification, analysis, planning responses, and monitoring and controlling risks in the project is part of which knowledge area?

   A. Project Risk Identification Management

   B. Project Risk Analysis Management

   C. Project Risk Management

   D. Project Risk Mitigation Management

18. You have been asked by the project sponsor to determine the best development life cycle for the new microwave cooking devices project and must ensure that customer value and quality are incorporated during development. What is your best course of action?

    A. Indicate that this is not a normal project manager decision, but you are willing to discuss the request with the project sponsor.

    B. Appoint a committee to investigate the idea and then interview key stakeholders about high-level business requirements.

    C. Draw a continuum of project life cycles, and consider the risk and cost of the initial planning effort.

    D. Choose an adaptive life cycle to bring focus to the customer value using agile, iterative, or incremental approaches.

1. C	**7.** D	**13.** D
2. B	**8.** A	**14.** C
3. D	**9.** A	**15.** C
4. B	**10.** B	**16.** A
5. B	**11.** C	**17.** C
6. C	**12.** C	**18.** D

1. Which knowledge area guides a project team in completing work that has been agreed upon with the project sponsor?

   A. Project Quality Management

   B. Project Change Management

   C. Project Scope Management

   D. Project Configuration Management

   ☑ **C.** As a part of understanding the five project management process groups and the processes within each group, a project manager knows that the project scope defines the agreed upon and approved work that the project delivers. Only this work should be done. Any changes to the project are managed by referring to the project scope first and then are carried out in the process defined by project change management.

   ☒ **A, B,** and **D** are incorrect because these are control processes used to ensure high-quality deliverables or to assist in approving changes to the project scope. However, it is scope management that governs the work that the team is authorized to complete.

2. In which process group does the project manager obtain, manage, and use resources to accomplish the project objectives?

   A. Initiating

   B. Executing

   C. Planning

   D. Monitoring and Controlling

   ☑ **B.** The purpose of the Executing process group is to obtain, manage, and use resources to accomplish project objectives.

   ☒ **A, C,** and **D** are incorrect. Only the Executing process group puts resources to use to accomplish project objectives. Initiating puts a project charter in place. Planning itemizes all the actions that will need to be taken in the Executing process. Monitoring and Control ensures that the work taking place in Executing is done correctly.

3. Which of the following is true of program and portfolio management?

   A. A project manager manages programs, portfolios, and projects.

   B. The objectives of programs, portfolios, and projects are the same.

   C. Programs, portfolios, and projects may share the same lifecycles.

   D. Stakeholders and resources may be the same in programs, portfolios, and projects.

   ☑ **D.** Portfolios, programs, projects, and operations can engage the same stakeholders and may need to make use of the same resources, even though it may cause conflict in the organization.

   ☒ **A, B,** and **C** are incorrect. **A** is incorrect because a project manager manages projects. **B** and **C** are incorrect because the objectives and life cycles are different between projects vs. programs vs. portfolios.

4. What is one of the goals of portfolio management?

    A. Minimize expenses across programs

    B. Manage multiple simultaneous projects

    C. Maximize profit between projects

    D. Mitigate the risks of stand-alone projects

    ☑ **B.** Portfolio management by an organization helps manage multiple programs and projects that are taking place at the same time.

    ☒ **A, C,** and **D** are incorrect. **A** and **C** are incorrect because the goal of portfolio management is focused on simultaneous programs and projects, not on simply minimizing expenses or maximizing profits of programs or projects without reference to whether they are simultaneous. **D** is incorrect because stand-alone projects have no relationship to other projects, and portfolio management does not focus on mitigating risks on an individual project.

5. The series of phases that a project passes through to create a product is best described as:

    A. Product life cycle

    B. Project life cycle

    C. Program life cycle

    D. Portfolio life cycle

    ☑ **B.** The project's life cycle is the series of phases a project follows from the project beginning until the project end.

    ☒ **A, B,** and **C** are incorrect. **A** is incorrect because a product is created from the project's phases, and the product will have its own life cycle. **B** and **C** are incorrect because program and portfolio life cycles do not describe the project phases.

6. Which process groups ensure that the project work is carried out?

    A. Planning and Executing

    B. Initiating and Closing

    C. Executing and Monitoring and Controlling

    D. Monitoring and Controlling

    ☑ **C.** Executing and Monitoring and Controlling are the project phases that occur during the time when the project work is carried out.

    ☒ **A, B,** and **D** are incorrect. **A** is incorrect because Planning is when a project manager organizes and prepares the work that will be carried out in the project. **B** is incorrect because Initiating is the starting of the project with no work activities yet defined, and Closing is the ending of the project following the completion of the work of the project. **D** is incorrect because it leaves out Executing.

7. Which of the following best describes a system of practices, techniques, procedures, and rules used by those who work in a particular discipline?

   A. Program

   B. Management

   C. Project

   D. Methodology

   ☑ **D.** A methodology is a system for working in a discipline. However, the *PMBOK Guide, Sixth Edition* is a guide to project management best practices and is *not* a methodology.

   ☒ **A**, **B**, and **C** are incorrect. Programs, management, and projects are not systems for working in a discipline and instead make use of and apply methodologies to their work.

8. Which of the following competing factors should be the focus of tailoring the project management phases in the PMBOK Guide for individual projects?

   A. Scope, schedule, cost, resources, quality, and risk

   B. Initiating and planning

   C. Risk management and procurement approaches

   D. Teams, managers, matrix, hierarchies, vendors, and collaboration

   ☑ **A.** For each project, the scope, schedule, cost, resources, quality, and risk will be unique. These are the factors that will be the focus of tailoring the project management phases for individual projects.

   ☒ **B**, **C**, and **D** are incorrect. **B** is incorrect because Initiating and Planning are phases that will be tailored based on the factors of scope, schedule, cost, resources, quality, and risk. **C** is incorrect because risk and procurement approaches will be tailored based on listed factors. **D** is incorrect because teams, managers, matrix, hierarchies, vendors, and collaboration may change with each project but are not the focus of tailoring the project management approach.

9. Which stakeholders make the tailoring decision for a project?

   A. Project manager and project sponsor

   B. Project sponsor and organizational management

   C. Project manager and business analyst

   D. The project team

   ☑ **A.** The project manager collaborates with some combination of the project team, the project sponsor, and the organizational management to make tailoring decisions for each project.

   ☒ **B**, **C**, and **D** are incorrect. **B** and **D** are incorrect because the project manager must be involved. **C** is incorrect because it names the business analyst who is part of the project team but is not the entire project team.

10. Which of the following activities would you undertake as a project manager to best understand the project environment?

A. Schedule all resources

B. Identify cultural and social issues

C. Project budget approval process

D. Detailed requirements analysis

☑ **B.** When planning and implementing a project, one of the considerations is the project environment, including the cultural and social issues that may affect the success of the project.

☒ **A, C,** and **D** are incorrect. They are specific details of the project rather than the project environment. Requirements are details that are evaluated later in the planning processes.

11. What is the function of the project management office?

A. Provide standard forms for project paperwork.

B. Close project accounts at the end of the projects.

C. Coordinate the management of projects.

D. Provide hot-desk facilities for all project managers.

☑ **C.** The project management office (PMO) exists to coordinate and support the management of projects in an organization. Processes, policies, and procedures are usually established by the PMO for use in all projects.

☒ **A, B,** and **D** are incorrect. **A** is incorrect because the PMO does not only provide standard forms. **B** is incorrect because it is the responsibility of the project manager to close a project. **D** is incorrect because the PMO is not necessarily responsible for hot desking.

12. What is the process called that defines and controls what is and is not included in a given project?

A. Project Documentation Management

B. Project Change Control

C. Plan Scope Management

D. Governance

☑ **C.** The Plan Scope Management process defines and controls what is and what is not included in the project.

☒ **A, B,** and **D** are incorrect. **A** and **B** are incorrect because Project Documentation Management and Project Change Control are procedures that allow the control of changes to scope only. **D** is incorrect because Governance is a process that controls how decisions on changes within a project are made.

13. In which process does a project team work together to define procedures by which the project scope and product scope can be modified?

    A. Validate Scope

    B. Plan Configuration Management

    C. Initial Scope Definition

    D. Control Scope

    ☑ **D.** Defining the procedures by which the project scope and product scope can be changed is known as Control Scope.

    ☒ **A, B,** and **C** are incorrect. **A** is incorrect because Validate Scope is done at the end of a project to confirm the deliverables are as contracted. **B** is incorrect because Configuration Management is the process of controlling requirements and considering changes before they are put into change control. **C** is incorrect because Initial Scope Definition sets the high-level scope at the beginning of a project but is silent on controlling how scope may be changed later during the project.

14. In which knowledge area does the project manager identify the activities, dependencies, and resources needed to produce the project deliverables?

    A. Project Schedule Control Management

    B. Project Risk Management

    C. Project Schedule Management

    D. Project Cost Planning Management

    ☑ **C.** Identifying the activities, dependencies, and resources needed to produce the project deliverables are some of the actions required in Project Schedule Management.

    ☒ **A, B,** and **D** are incorrect. Only Schedule Management is concerned with managing the activities, dependencies, and resources. Project Schedule Control is about managing changes to the schedule. Project Risk Management activities focus on identifying and planning mitigation for risk. Cost Planning is about the specific financials of a project.

15. Determining the cost of the resources needed to complete the planned schedule of activities on a project is called

    A. Project Risk Management

    B. Project Schedule Management

    C. Project Cost Management

    D. Project Resource Management

    ☑ **C.** Project activity work that looks at the cost of the resources needed to complete the planned schedule of activities on a project is the knowledge area called Project Cost Management.

⊠ **A**, **B**, and **D** are incorrect. **A** is incorrect because Project Risk Management is the knowledge area focused on risks, not solely on costs. **B** is incorrect because Schedule Management is concerned with the duration and dependencies of tasks. **D** is incorrect because the Project Resource Management knowledge area identifies necessary resources and checks that are available, but does not focus on the cost.

16. Which of the following describes the work of monitoring and recording the results of executing quality activities to assess performance and recommend necessary changes?

    A. Control Quality

    B. Perform Quality Assurance

    C. Plan Quality

    D. Quality Improvement

    ☑ **A.** The definition of the Control Quality process is monitoring and recording results of executing quality activities to assess performance and recommend necessary changes.

    ⊠ **B**, **C**, and **D** are incorrect. **B** is incorrect because Perform Quality Assurance is ensuring that appropriate quality standards are used. **C** is incorrect because Plan Quality is establishing the requirements and/or standards for the project. **D** is incorrect because Quality Improvement is an organizational development process.

17. The set of project management activities that includes identification, analysis, planning responses, and monitoring and controlling risks in the project is part of which knowledge area?

    A. Project Risk Identification Management

    B. Project Risk Analysis Management

    C. Project Risk Management

    D. Project Risk Mitigation Management

    ☑ **C.** Identification, analysis, planning responses, and monitoring and controlling of risks in the project are part of the Project Risk Management knowledge area.

    ⊠ **A**, **B**, and **D** are incorrect. Risk identification, analysis, and mitigation are all parts of the overall process of Project Risk Management.

18. You have been asked by the project sponsor to determine the best development life cycle for the new microwave cooking devices project and must ensure that customer value and quality are incorporated during development. What is your best course of action?

    A. Indicate that this is not a normal project manager decision, but you are willing to discuss the request with the project sponsor.

    B. Appoint a committee to investigate the idea and then interview key stakeholders about high-level business requirements.

C. Draw a continuum of project life cycles, and consider the risk and cost of the initial planning effort.

D. Choose an adaptive life cycle to bring focus to the customer value using agile, iterative, or incremental approaches.

☑ **D.** An adaptive approach is a tailoring option in project management that puts a focus on collaborative decision making with the customer to ensure the value the customer desires is built into the project.

☒ **A, B,** and **C** are incorrect. **A** is incorrect because it is normal for the project manager and the project management team to determine the best life cycle for each project. **B** is incorrect because appointing a committee to investigate the idea and then interviewing key stakeholders about high-level business requirements does not fit with the project manager's roles in the sphere of influence. **C** is incorrect because drawing a continuum of project life cycles and considering the risk and cost of the initial planning effort depend on the life cycle being employed.

Project Environment

In this chapter, you will

- Identify the factors and assets that may impact the outcome of a project
- Distinguish between organizational systems
- Understand the purpose and activities of a Project Management Office
- Recognize the hierarchy of projects, programs and portfolios

Chapter 2 of the *PMBOK Guide, Sixth Edition*, "The Environment in Which Projects Operate," accounts for 6 percent (18) of the questions on the CAPM exam.

Projects are not completed in a vacuum, devoid of influence by organizational process assets (OPAs) and enterprise environmental factors (EEFs), structure types (matrix, projectized, hybrid, etc.), and governance framework (e.g., PMO). It is important for a project manager to recognize that each of these elements can positively or negatively influence the outcome of a project.

The environment in which a project operates is a direct reflection of the level of maturity of the organization.

The 18 practice questions in this chapter are mapped to the style and frequency of question types you will see on the CAPM exam.

1. What is the best role for a project management office in an organization with a low level of project management maturity?

   A. Directive

   B. Controlling

   C. Supportive

   D. Enabling

2. The CEO of your organization is considering the strategic reasons the company has for approving your project proposal. At times he seems confused about what exactly a strategic consideration is. Which of the following is not a strategic consideration for authorizing a project?

   A. Strategic opportunity

   B. Return on investment

   C. Customer demand

   D. Market demand

3. The team or function assigned responsibility for the centralized and coordinated management of projects within an organization is known as what?

   A. Project headquarters

   B. Program management office

   C. Project management office

   D. War room

4. Which of the following is not a primary function of a project management office?

   A. Providing a project manager with daily progress reports on a specific project

   B. Managing shared resources across several projects

   C. Identifying and developing project management methodologies, best practices, and standards

   D. Coordinating communication across projects

5. Which of the following examples would not be considered an enterprise environmental factor?

   A. Government or industry standards or regulations

   B. Political climate

   C. Net present value of investment

   D. Organizational structure

6. The internal and external environmental factors that both surround and influence, and sometimes constrain, a project are known as what?

   A. Enterprise organizational assets

   B. Environmental process assets

   C. Environmental enterprise constraints

   D. Enterprise environmental factors

7. The type of organization where the functional manager controls the project budget and resource availability is commonly referred to as what?

   A. Projectized

   B. Strong matrix

   C. Functional

   D. Weak matrix

8. In an organization where staff members are grouped according to their specialty, such as production, engineering, and accounting, and projects are generally undertaken within these respective groupings, what is the organizational structure known as?

   A. Projectized

   B. Weak matrix

   C. Strong matrix

   D. Functional

9. All the following are examples of organizational process assets (OPAs) that can assist your project except?

   A. Government regulations

   B. Lessons learned from previous projects

   C. A template for a work breakdown structure

   D. Configuration management knowledge bases

10. Your organization has implemented best practices in project management processes. One function that has been set up is the project management office (PMO). What is the function of the PMO?

    A. Provide hot-desk facilities for all project managers

    B. Coordinate the management of projects

    C. Close project accounts at the end of the projects

    D. Provide standard stationery for project paperwork

11. Which of the following organizational structures can complicate the management of the project team?

   A. Functional

   B. Matrix

   C. Project

   D. Hierarchical

12. To be successful in a weak matrix environment, you need to:

   A. Get commitments in writing that the functional manager will allocate the team member to your project for two years

   B. Encourage the project team to collaborate/problem-solve to build consensus and commitment

   C. Give certificates of appreciation to the functional team members at key milestone points to influence them to stay on the project

   D. Have each team member sign a letter of intent stating that he or she will stay on the project until completion

13. When a project is established, which of the following is least likely to be involved in developing governance for project tracking and updating?

   A. Project board

   B. Project managers

   C. Project office

   D. Project management office (PMO)

14. You are a project manager and are periodically verifying that team leaders are adhering to established project management methodologies and delivering products that meet business and technical requirements. What major project management theme do these activities most support?

   A. Manage quality

   B. Stakeholder engagement

   C. Project governance

   D. Benefits delivery

15. Which process group or process provides the most primary interface with the project governance structure?

   A. Executing

   B. Monitoring and Controlling

   C. Direct and Manage Project Work

   D. Monitor and Control Project Work

16. You have issued a change request, and because it requires corrective action beyond your approval level, your next step is to:

    A. Schedule a meeting with your PMO

    B. Receive governance approval to proceed

    C. Set up a change control board to see if the change should be implemented

    D. Use your project management information system (PMIS)

17. Awareness of the diverse population in your project will benefit least from which of the following?

    A. Describing the organization's culture

    B. Describing the team structure and individual cultures

    C. Maintaining cohesiveness among all teams

    D. Establishing workgroups that consist of individual cultural groups

18. You are leading and performing the work defined in the project management plan. Which of the following actions would be least helpful to you?

    A. Allocate available resources

    B. Manage organizational interfaces

    C. Analyze work performance data

    D. Leverage prior organizational knowledge

1. C	**7.** D	**13.** B
2. B	**8.** D	**14.** C
3. C	**9.** A	**15.** B
4. A	**10.** B	**16.** B
5. C	**11.** B	**17.** D
6. D	**12.** B	**18.** D

1. What is the best role for a project management office in an organization with a low level of project management maturity?

   A. Directive

   B. Controlling

   C. Supportive

   D. Enabling

   ☑ **C.** Supportive project management offices are generally a sign of a low level of project management maturity, because they do not support a lot of complexity.

   ☒ **A**, **B**, and **D** are incorrect. **A** is incorrect because directive project management offices are generally best in an organization with a high level of project management maturity. **B** is incorrect because controlling project management offices are generally a sign of an organization improving its organizational project management maturity. **D** is incorrect because this is a made-up term and is not from the *PMBOK Guide.*

2. The CEO of your organization is considering the strategic reasons the company has for approving your project proposal. At times he seems confused about what exactly a strategic consideration is. Which of the following is not a strategic consideration for authorizing a project?

   A. Strategic opportunity

   B. Return on investment

   C. Customer demand

   D. Market demand

   ☑ **B.** Return on investment is not a strategic consideration. It is a method of calculating whether a project should proceed from a financial rather than a strategic point of view.

   ☒ **A**, **C**, and **D** are incorrect. **A** is incorrect because the chance to achieve a strategic opportunity is a clear strategic consideration for authorizing a project. **C** is incorrect because customer demand is a strategic consideration because it is a forecast of what the customer will want in the future, and the company's strategic goals should include the desire to fulfill this demand. **D** is incorrect because market demand is a strategic consideration because it is a forecast of how the market will be behaving in the future, and the company's strategic goals should include the desire to fulfill this demand.

3. The team or function assigned responsibility for the centralized and coordinated management of projects within an organization is known as what?

   A. Project headquarters

   B. Program management office

   C. Project management office

   D. War room

   ☑ **C.** A project management office (PMO) takes responsibility for providing organization-wide project management support functions, including common standards, templates, and processes. It is also directly responsible for project delivery.

   ☒ **A**, **B**, and **D** are incorrect. **A** is incorrect because project headquarters is not correct; although the term may be used by some organizations, it is not part of the standardized terminology offered by the *PMBOK Guide*. **B** is incorrect because although sometimes the acronym PMO does stand for program management office, it is more commonly used to refer to a project management office, which is the more correct answer in this instance. **D** is incorrect because a war room is a specific meeting room for project team members to be co-located and focus on doing the project work.

4. Which of the following is not a primary function of a project management office?

   A. Providing a project manager with daily progress reports on a specific project

   B. Managing shared resources across several projects

   C. Identifying and developing project management methodologies, best practices, and standards

   D. Coordinating communication across projects

   ☑ **A.** A PMO provides high-level support across several projects. It does not provide lower-level detail to a single project but would instead provide a rolled-up summary report of the project.

   ☒ **B**, **C**, and **D** are incorrect. **B** is incorrect because a clear role of a mature PMO would be to oversee and manage shared resources across several projects. **C** is incorrect because one role of a PMO is to develop and improve an organization's project management methodology. **D** is incorrect because one very clear role of any sort of PMO is to ensure communications across projects is done effectively.

5. Which of the following examples would not be considered an enterprise environmental factor?

   A. Government or industry standards or regulations

   B. Political climate

   C. Net present value of investment

   D. Organizational structure

☑ **C.** Net present value of investment is a tool for project selection.

☒ **A**, **B**, and **D** are incorrect. **A** is incorrect because government standards and industry regulations are a great example of enterprise environmental factors, as they can affect a project. **B** is incorrect because the political climate that a project operates in is an enterprise environmental factor. **D** is incorrect because organizational structure is an example of internal enterprise environmental factors.

6. The internal and external environmental factors that both surround and influence, and sometimes constrain, a project are known as what?

   A. Enterprise organizational assets

   B. Environmental process assets

   C. Environmental enterprise constraints

   D. Enterprise environmental factors

   ☑ **D.** Enterprise environmental factors (EEFs) are a fairly constant input into many of the processes. They can be thought of as the environment in which the project must operate and by which it will be influenced.

   ☒ **A**, **B**, and **C** are incorrect. The answers are not terms referenced within the *PMBOK Guide*.

7. The type of organization where the functional manager controls the project budget and resource availability is commonly referred to as what?

   A. Projectized

   B. Strong matrix

   C. Functional

   D. Weak matrix

   ☑ **D.** This situation describes a matrix organization where the functional manager retains most of the power. Therefore, it is a weak matrix, reflecting the small amount of power the project manager has to influence resources and budget on the project.

   ☒ **A**, **B**, and **C** are incorrect. **A** is incorrect because in a projectized structure the project manager would have full responsibility and authority. **B** is incorrect because in a strong matrix, the project manager, not the functional manager, would have the most power. **C** is incorrect because this question refers to some staff working for you, implying there are other staff from other functional areas working for you, which indicates a matrix form of organization—specifically a weak matrix.

8. In an organization where staff members are grouped according to their specialty, such as production, engineering, and accounting, and projects are generally undertaken within these respective groupings, what is the organizational structure known as?

   A. Projectized

   B. Weak matrix

   C. Strong matrix

   D. Functional

   ☑ **D.** This situation describes an organization divided into its functional responsibilities. A project manager will often have to deal with staff and resources from different areas across the organization that are ultimately controlled by the functional manager. As such, the project manager has little or no power in this type of organization.

   ☒ **A**, **B**, and **C** are incorrect. **A** is incorrect because in a projectized structure, the project manager would have full responsibility and authority. **B** is incorrect because a weak matrix would be a matrix organization where the project manager has less power than a functional manager but still has some. **C** is incorrect because a strong matrix would be a matrix organization where the project manager has more power than the functional manager.

9. All the following are examples of organizational process assets (OPAs) that can assist your project except?

   A. Government regulations

   B. Lessons learned from previous projects

   C. A template for a work breakdown structure

   D. Configuration management knowledge bases

   ☑ **A.** Government regulations are an example of enterprise environmental factors. The other three are examples of organizational process assets, which belong to the company, are the property of the company, and reflect the organizational culture.

   ☒ **B**, **C**, and **D** are incorrect. **B** is incorrect because lessons learned are an example of organizational process assets, owned by the organization and used to assist projects. **C** is incorrect because any template used to assist projects is an example of organizational process assets. **D** is incorrect because configuration management knowledge bases are an example of organizational process assets.

10. Your organization has implemented best practices in project management processes. One function that has been set up is the project management office (PMO). What is the function of the PMO?

    A. Provide hot-desk facilities for all project managers

    B. Coordinate the management of projects

    C. Close project accounts at the end of the projects

    D. Provide standard stationery for project paperwork

☑ **B.** One of the functions of the PMO is to coordinate the management of projects.

☒ **A**, **C**, and **D** are incorrect. **A** is incorrect because the PMO is not responsible for hot-desk implementation. **C** is incorrect because the project manager is responsible for closure of all project accounts. **D** is incorrect because items like stationery are project resources, not a function of a PMO.

11. Which of the following organizational structures can complicate the management of the project team?

   A. Functional

   B. Matrix

   C. Project

   D. Hierarchical

   ☑ **B.** Management of the project team is complicated when team members are accountable to both a functional and a project manager, as in a matrix organization.

   ☒ **A**, **C**, and **D** are incorrect. Functional and project organizations have clear accountability. Hierarchical organizations are the norm.

12. To be successful in a weak matrix environment, you need to:

   A. Get commitments in writing that the functional manager will allocate the team member to your project for two years

   B. Encourage the project team to collaborate/problem-solve to build consensus and commitment

   C. Give certificates of appreciation to the functional team members at key milestone points to influence them to stay on the project

   D. Have each team member sign a letter of intent stating that he or she will stay on the project until completion

   ☑ **B.** Encouraging collaborative problem solving improves consensus and commitment to the team. It also creates a cohesive team culture.

   ☒ **A**, **C**, and **D** are incorrect. **A** is incorrect because even if the functional manager commits in writing to allocating the team member to your project, there is still no guarantee the commitment would be honored when business/strategy changes. **C** is incorrect because certificates of appreciation will only be effective if they satisfy a need that is valued by that individual. **D** is incorrect because a letter of intent (LOI) is a document outlining the general plans of an agreement between two or more parties before a legal agreement is finalized. A letter of intent is not a contract and cannot be legally enforced. However, it can signify a serious commitment from one involved party to another.

13. When a project is established, which of the following is least likely to be involved in developing governance for project tracking and updating?

    A. Project board

    B. Project managers

    C. Project office

    D. Project management office (PMO)

    ☑ **B.** When you are establishing a management infrastructure, you must set up governance for all projects within the organization. This normally includes a project board, project management office, and project teams. Project managers are not normally involved directly with setting up governance for the project. Project managers execute and apply project governance as defined by the project management office.

    ☒ **A**, **C**, and **D** are incorrect. **A** is incorrect because the project board is part of organizational governance. **C** and **D** are incorrect because both refer to the project management office, which is involved in organizational governance for projects.

14. You are a project manager and are periodically verifying that team leaders are adhering to established project management methodologies and delivering products that meet business and technical requirements. What major project management theme do these activities most support?

    A. Manage quality

    B. Stakeholder engagement

    C. Project governance

    D. Benefits delivery

    ☑ **C.** Project governance focuses on oversight of the project. This is carried out through phase gate reviews to aid in project control and provides an objective check against exit criteria.

    ☒ **A**, **B**, and **D** are incorrect. Each is unrelated to verifying that team leaders are following project management methodologies.

15. Which process group or process provides the most primary interface with the project governance structure?

    A. Executing

    B. Monitoring and Controlling

    C. Direct and Manage Project Work

    D. Monitor and Control Project Work

☑ **B**. The Monitoring and Controlling process group is where the project manager obtains and consolidates status and progress data from project work packages, interfaces with the project governance structure, and reports on project performance.

☒ **A**, **C**, and **D** are incorrect. **A** is incorrect because project governance is most prevalent in the Monitoring and Controlling process group. **C** is incorrect because Direct and Manage Project Work is the process of leading and performing the work defined in the project management plan and implementing approved changes to achieve the project's objectives. **D** is incorrect because the proper name is Monitor and Control Project Work.

16. You have issued a change request, and because it requires corrective action beyond your approval level, your next step is to:

    A. Schedule a meeting with your PMO

    B. Receive governance approval to proceed

    C. Set up a change control board to see if the change should be implemented

    D. Use your project management information system (PMIS)

    ☑ **B**. Governance is the framework within which authority is exercised in organizations. This framework includes policies, procedures, and approval levels.

    ☒ **A**, **C**, and **D** are incorrect. **A** is incorrect because the PMO standardizes the project-related governance processes. **C** is incorrect because the change control board is responsible for deciding what to do with change requests. **D** is incorrect because the PMIS is used for the outputs of project management processes.

17. Awareness of the diverse population in your project will benefit least from which of the following?

    A. Describing the organization's culture

    B. Describing the team structure and individual cultures

    C. Maintaining cohesiveness among all teams

    D. Establishing workgroups that consist of individual cultural groups

    ☑ **D**. Motivating the team using appropriate tools and techniques to increase commitment to the project deliverables requires you to have knowledge of diversity awareness and be able to describe the organization's culture, describe the team structure and individual cultures, establish a safe and secure work environment, and maintain cohesiveness among all teams.

    ☒ **A**, **B**, and **C** are incorrect because they are each components of creating an awareness of the diverse population.

18. You are leading and performing the work defined in the project management plan. Which of the following actions would be least helpful to you?

A. Allocate available resources

B. Manage organizational interfaces

C. Analyze work performance data

D. Leverage prior organizational knowledge

☑ **D.** The question is asking about the Direct and Manage Project Work process. Leveraging prior organizational knowledge is considered part of the expert judgment technique.

☒ **A**, **B**, and **C** are incorrect. They are all project activities to complete project deliverables and accomplish established objectives.

Role of the Project Manager

In this chapter, you will

- State the primary functions of a project manager
- Understand a project manager's sphere of influence
- Identify the major elements included in the PMI triangle
- Recognize the difference between leadership and management

For a project to be successful, the project manager must take a leadership role in guiding the project from inception to closure. Along the way, a project manager plans the project budget, plans the project activities, monitors the project activities that were planned, reports on the project work, and engages with management outside the project and team members inside the project. Certified Associate in Project Management (CAPM) candidates are tested on four objectives that emphasize the candidate's understanding of the variety of duties performed and the responsibility given to the project manager.

The 21 practice questions in this chapter are mapped to the style and frequency of question types you will see on the CAPM exam.

1. Which project role is generally accountable for the development and maintenance of the business case associated with a project?

   A. Project sponsor

   B. Project manager

   C. Business stakeholder

   D. IT stakeholder

2. Which of the following statements best describes the role of the project manager?

   A. Implement the business goals

   B. Create the measurable KPIs for the project

   C. Lead the team in achieving project objectives

   D. Carry out the directives from the project sponsor

3. How is the success of a project manager measured?

   A. By completing the project on time

   B. By achieving the project objectives

   C. By building the right product

   D. By developing the talents of the team

4. Which of the following is a true statement regarding the project management role?

   A. The role of project manager must be filled by someone who is certified as a project manager.

   B. The role of project manager is the same as the role of the business analyst.

   C. The role of the project manager is tailored to fit the organization.

   D. The role of the project manager is limited to Initiating, Planning, Executing, Monitoring and Controlling, and Closing a project.

5. Who is responsible for what project team members produce?

   A. Each team member's functional manager is responsible for their employee's contributions to the team.

   B. The project manager is responsible for what the project team produces.

   C. Human resources is responsible for each team member's contribution and tracks such for performance appraisal purposes.

   D. The project's quality manager is responsible for the work created by the project team.

6. How is the role of functional manager different from the role of project manager?

   A. A functional manager focuses on leading project teams in the business function, while a project manager leads project teams in the technical side of a company.

   B. A project manager focuses on operations and the work of the company, while a functional manager leads business teams to create business requirements.

C. A project manager focuses on implementation details for development teams, while a functional manager focuses on requirements and designs.

D. A functional manager focuses on providing management oversight for a functional or business unit, while a project manager focuses on leading a project team to complete project objectives.

7. How many levels are in a project manager's sphere of influence?

   A. 1

   B. 2

   C. 3

   D. 4

8. Which of the following demonstrates a project manager's sphere of influence over the project?

   A. Influencing end users

   B. Influencing governing bodies

   C. Influencing the project team

   D. Influencing the project sponsor

9. Which of the following is an example of a project manager's sphere of influence over the organization?

   A. Interacting with other project managers

   B. Staying current with industry trends

   C. Participating in training

   D. Contributing knowledge and expertise at the global level

10. Which two essential skills are used by the top 2 percent of successful project managers consistently and effectively?

   A. Technical skills and superior time management skills

   B. Business acumen and political influence

   C. Superior relationship and communication skills

   D. Strategy analysis skills and solution evaluation skills

11. Which of the following is a way a project manager can create positive influence given independent project demands on the same resources sought by the project manager?

   A. Escalating project needs to the PMO

   B. Seeking additional funding early in a project

   C. Running tasks in parallel in the project

   D. Developing relationships with other project managers

12. As the project manager, which stakeholder do you interact with to address internal political and strategic issues that may affect your project team?

    A. Project management office

    B. Project sponsor

    C. Project business analyst

    D. All stakeholders

13. What is the difference between leadership and management?

    A. Leadership is about demonstrating the value of project management.

    B. Management is about delivering better strategic outcomes.

    C. Leadership includes making sure the project is delivered on target, on schedule, and on budget.

    D. Leadership involves guiding, motivating, and directing the project team.

14. According to *Navigating Complexity: A Practice Guide,* the three dimensions of complexity are:

    A. Systems thinking, creative thinking, and problem solving

    B. Goals, objectives, and requirements

    C. System behavior, human behavior, and ambiguity

    D. Tacit knowledge, explicit knowledge, and experiential knowledge

15. How does a project manager treat the aspect of politics in an organization?

    A. By exerting political influence from a project into the functional or matrix management structure

    B. By reacting to negative political pressures on the project from outside the project

    C. By minimizing the influence that politics has on the project

    D. By understanding how the organization works, the project manager is more likely to be successful

16. Which of the following combines influence, negotiation, autonomy, and power?

    A. Politics

    B. Conflict resolution

    C. Project initiation

    D. Strategy analysis

17. The skills of a leader include the ability to manage relationships and conflict. Which quality is critical to this skill?

   A. Choosing the best team

   B. Building trust

   C. Creating a give-and-take relationship with the project sponsor

   D. Establishing two-way communication with the project sponsor

18. Based on research, what percentage of time do top managers spend communicating during a project?

   A. 50 percent

   B. 70 percent

   C. 85 percent

   D. 90 percent

19. A project manager who exhibits the ability to guide, motivate, and direct a team is demonstrating what type of skill?

   A. Project management

   B. Leadership

   C. Negotiation

   D. Problem solving

20. A project manager who is participating in training, continuing education, and development is demonstrating which aspect of project management?

   A. Knowledge transfer and integration

   B. Training future project managers

   C. Learning business analysis techniques

   D. Collecting the right number of PDUs in a one-year cycle

21. Which of the following skill sets does a project manager demonstrate when exhibiting knowledge of and expertise in the industry and the organization with a focus on better outcomes?

   A. Technical project management

   B. Generic project management

   C. Leadership and research

   D. Strategic and business management

1. A	**8.** C	**15.** D
2. C	**9.** A	**16.** A
3. B	**10.** C	**17.** B
4. C	**11.** D	**18.** D
5. B	**12.** B	**19.** B
6. D	**13.** D	**20.** A
7. C	**14.** C	**21.** D

1. Which project role is generally accountable for the development and maintenance of the business case associated with a project?

   A. Project sponsor

   B. Project manager

   C. Business stakeholder

   D. IT stakeholder

   ☑ **A.** The project sponsor is responsible for funding the project and ensuring that it takes place. A business analyst may assist in writing the business case, but the project sponsor is accountable for the deliverable.

   ☒ **B, C,** and **D** are incorrect. **B** is incorrect because the business case precedes the project charter, which links a project manager to a project. **C** and **D** are incorrect because although either may be in the role of project sponsor, in which case they would be responsible, this would only be in the role of business or IT stakeholder—there is no power to authorize a project.

2. Which of the following statements best describes the role of the project manager?

   A. Implement the business goals

   B. Create the measurable KPIs for the project

   C. Lead the team in achieving project objectives

   D. Carry out the directives from the project sponsor

   ☑ **C.** The project is assigned to the project manager by the performing organization to lead the team responsible for achieving the project objectives.

   ☒ **A, B,** and **D** are incorrect. **A** is incorrect because implementing the business goals is the responsibilities of all company employees and is not isolated to the project manager. **B** is incorrect because while key performance indicators (KPIs) are helpful to measure progress, KPIs can be created by the project team as a whole as well as the organization itself. **D** is incorrect because while the project sponsor is the original source for identifying the business need, the word *directives* implies that the sponsor can direct the project manager to do tasks that may not be related to the business need, and this is not the case.

3. How is the success of a project manager measured?

   A. By completing the project on time

   B. By achieving the project objectives

   C. By building the right product

   D. By developing the talents of the team

   ☑ **B.** A project manager is successful when the project objectives have been achieved and the stakeholders are satisfied.

☒ **A**, **C**, and **D** are incorrect. **A** is incorrect because completing a project on time is but one variable a project manager is responsible for—a project that completes on time but does not achieve the project objectives is not a success. **C** is incorrect because building the right project is important but if other variables are compromised (timeline, budget), then the project objectives have not been met. **D** is incorrect because while developing the talents of the team is important, meeting the project objectives is more important.

4. Which of the following is a true statement regarding the project management role?

   A. The role of project manager must be filled by someone who is certified as a project manager.

   B. The role of project manager is the same as the role of the business analyst.

   C. The role of the project manager is tailored to fit the organization.

   D. The role of the project manager is limited to Initiating, Planning, Executing, Monitoring and Controlling, and Closing a project.

   ☑ **C.** Just as the project management processes are tailored to fit the project, the role of the project manager is tailored to fit the organization.

   ☒ **A**, **B**, and **D** are incorrect. **A** is incorrect because project management certification is advisable but is not mandatory. **B** is incorrect because the project manager is responsible for the project, while the business analyst is responsible for specifying the product requirements. **D** is incorrect because a project manager may also be involved in the strategy analysis before a project begins and in the solution evaluation after a solution is created by the project.

5. Who is responsible for what project team members produce?

   A. Each team member's functional manager is responsible for their employee's contributions to the team.

   B. The project manager is responsible for what the project team produces.

   C. Human resources is responsible for each team member's contribution and tracks such for performance appraisal purposes.

   D. The project's quality manager is responsible for the work created by the project team.

   ☑ **B.** Like an orchestra conductor, the project manager is responsible for the project outcome the team produces.

   ☒ **A**, **C**, and **D** are incorrect. The functional manager in a matrix organization is responsible for the employee's career growth and HR is responsible for staffing, but neither is responsible for the product being created by the employee as a part of the project. A project's quality manager is responsible for the quality of the product.

6. How is the role of functional manager different from the role of project manager?

   A. A functional manager focuses on leading project teams in the business function, while a project manager leads project teams in the technical side of a company.

   B. A project manager focuses on operations and the work of the company, while a functional manager leads business teams to create business requirements.

   C. A project manager focuses on implementation details for development teams, while a functional manager focuses on requirements and designs.

   D. A functional manager focuses on providing management oversight for a functional or business unit, while a project manager focuses on leading a project team to complete project objectives.

   ☑ **D.** A functional manager focuses on providing management oversight for a functional or business unit, while the project manager leads the team that is responsible for achieving project objectives.

   ☒ **A, B,** and **C** are incorrect. None of these answers identifies that the project manager is the person responsible for leading the team that is in turn responsible for achieving a project's objectives.

7. How many levels are in a project manager's sphere of influence?

   A. 1

   B. 2

   C. 3

   D. 4

   ☑ **C.** There are three levels in the sphere of influence for a project manager: those over which they directly influence, those that are outside the project and not considered stakeholders of the project, and those that are considered stakeholders of the project.

   ☒ **A, B,** and **D** are incorrect. There are three levels in the sphere of influence for a project manager: those over which they directly influence, those that are outside the project and not considered stakeholders of the project, and those that are considered stakeholders of the project.

8. Which of the following demonstrates a project manager's sphere of influence over the project?

   A. Influencing end users

   B. Influencing governing bodies

   C. Influencing the project team

   D. Influencing the project sponsor

☑ **C.** A project manager has direct influence over the project team and resource managers.

☒ **A, B,** and **D** are incorrect. **A** is incorrect because a project manager seeks to understand project stakeholders but does not influence them because they are outside the project team. **B** is incorrect because governing bodies influence the project manager, not the other way around. **D** is incorrect because like governing bodies, the project manager is influenced by the sponsor, who is not a part of the project team.

9. Which of the following is an example of a project manager's sphere of influence over the organization?

   A. Interacting with other project managers

   B. Staying current with industry trends

   C. Participating in training

   D. Contributing knowledge and expertise at the global level

   ☑ **A.** By proactively interacting with project managers, the project manager can influence the organization in situations where other independent projects may affect their own project.

   ☒ **B, C,** and **D** are incorrect because staying current with industry trends, participating in training, and contributing knowledge at the global level are all outside of influencing the current organization.

10. Which two essential skills are used by the top 2 percent of successful project managers consistently and effectively?

    A. Technical skills and superior time management skills

    B. Business acumen and political influence

    C. Superior relationship and communication skills

    D. Strategy analysis skills and solution evaluation skills

    ☑ **C.** Research shows that project managers who are in the top 2 percent of successful project managers have mastered excellent relationship and communication skills in addition to having a positive attitude.

    ☒ **A, B,** and **D** are incorrect. **A** is incorrect because while technical skills are important to the project manager, successful project managers have excellent relationship and communication skills in addition to having a positive attitude. **B** is incorrect because while business acumen and political influence may be helpful, they are not essential. **D** is incorrect because strategy analysis and solution evaluation skills are business analyst skills.

11. Which of the following is a way a project manager can create positive influence given independent project demands on the same resources sought by the project manager?

    A. Escalating project needs to the PMO

    B. Seeking additional funding early in a project

C. Running tasks in parallel in the project

D. Developing relationships with other project managers

☑ **D.** Interacting with other project managers helps to create a positive influence for fulfilling human, technical, and financial resource needs of the project. Seeking to develop relationships with other project managers can help the team.

☒ **A**, **B**, and **C** are incorrect. **A** is incorrect because escalating to the project management office (PMO) should be a path explored only after interacting directly with the competing project's manager. **B** is incorrect because while seeking additional funding early in a project is a good idea if the need for funding is anticipated, additional funding may not solve the problem of the same person being needed by more than one project during the exact same time period unless the funding is used to train or hire an alternative resource (which the question and answer do not imply). **C** is incorrect because running tasks in parallel in a single project does not diminish the need for the same resource needed by the competing project.

12. As the project manager, which stakeholder do you interact with to address internal political and strategic issues that may affect your project team?

   A. Project management office

   B. Project sponsor

   C. Project business analyst

   D. All stakeholders

   ☑ **B.** A project's sponsor is typically a high-level advocate for the project who approves funding for the project and therefore has insight into the political and strategic issues a project may encounter.

   ☒ **A**, **C**, and **D** are incorrect. **A** is incorrect because the PMO establishes processes, policies, and procedures used by all projects in a company, which is different from political and strategic insight. **C** is incorrect because the project business analyst is focused on the requirements for the project, which is tactical in nature. **D** is incorrect because not all stakeholders are responsible for political nuances and strategy of a company.

13. What is the difference between leadership and management?

   A. Leadership is about demonstrating the value of project management.

   B. Management is about delivering better strategic outcomes.

   C. Leadership includes making sure the project is delivered on target, on schedule, and on budget.

   D. Leadership involves guiding, motivating, and directing the project team.

   ☑ **D.** Leadership involves working with others through discussion or debate to guide them from one point to another.

☒ **A**, **B**, and **C** are incorrect. **A** is incorrect because management is about demonstrating the value of project management. **B** is incorrect because leadership is about delivering better strategic outcomes. **C** is incorrect because project management is the art and science of getting the project done—on target, on schedule, and on budget.

14. According to *Navigating Complexity: A Practice Guide,* the three dimensions of complexity are:

   A. Systems thinking, creative thinking, and problem solving

   B. Goals, objectives, and requirements

   C. System behavior, human behavior, and ambiguity

   D. Tacit knowledge, explicit knowledge, and experiential knowledge

   ☑ **C.** *Navigating Complexity: A Practice Guide* cites the dimensions of complexity as the interdependencies of components and systems, the interplay between diverse individuals and groups, and the uncertainty of emerging issues and lack of understanding or confusion.

   ☒ **A**, **B**, and **D** are incorrect. **A** is incorrect because these are examples of analytical thinking and problem solving. **B** is incorrect because goals, objectives, and requirements are components of strategy but not of complexity. **D** is incorrect because tacit, explicit, and experiential are types of knowledge held by subject matter experts but are not directly related to complexity.

15. How does a project manager treat the aspect of politics in an organization?

   A. By exerting political influence from a project into the functional or matrix management structure

   B. By reacting to negative political pressures on the project from outside the project

   C. By minimizing the influence that politics has on the project

   D. By understanding how the organization works, the project manager is more likely to be successful

   ☑ **D.** Political aspects are not good, bad, positive, or negative all by themselves, and this means that a project manager who understands how the organization works can integrate the political aspects of a project successfully.

   ☒ **A**, **B**, and **C** are incorrect. **A** is incorrect because projects do not have political influence. **B** is incorrect because political pressures are not always negative. **C** is incorrect because a project manager would not want to minimize positive political influence.

16. Which of the following combines influence, negotiation, autonomy, and power?

   A. Politics

   B. Conflict resolution

   C. Project initiation

   D. Strategy analysis

☑ **A.** Politics involves influence, negotiation, autonomy, and power.

☒ **B, C,** and **D** are incorrect. **B** is incorrect because conflict resolution is defined as a skill useful in reaching consensus inside and outside a team. **C** is incorrect because Project Initiation is a project management phase, and is not the definition of politics. **D** is incorrect because strategy analysis is the work done to fully understand the business need in order to initiate a project.

17. The skills of a leader include the ability to manage relationships and conflict. Which quality is critical to this skill?

  A. Choosing the best team

  B. Building trust

  C. Creating a give-and-take relationship with the project sponsor

  D. Establishing two-way communication with the project sponsor

  ☑ **B.** Building trust is an underlying aspect of managing relationships and conflict. Other aspects are satisfying concerns; seeking consensus; balancing competing and opposing goals; using persuasion, compromise, and conflict resolution skills; developing and nurturing personal and professional networks; taking a long-term view; and continuously developing and applying political acumen.

  ☒ **A, C,** and **D** are incorrect. **A** is incorrect because not all managers choose a team—some inherit a team—and they still have to be able to manage relationships and conflict. **C** is incorrect because managing conflicts and relationships happens between the project managers and stakeholders other than the project sponsor. **D** is incorrect because leadership is not focused on just the relationship with the project sponsor.

18. Based on research, what percentage of time do top managers spend communicating during a project?

  A. 50 percent

  B. 70 percent

  C. 85 percent

  D. 90 percent

  ☑ **D.** Research shows that top project managers spend about 90 percent of their time in communicating while on a project.

  ☒ **A, B,** and **C** are incorrect because research shows that top project managers spend about 90 percent of their time in communicating while on a project.

19. A project manager who exhibits the ability to guide, motivate, and direct a team is demonstrating what type of skill?

  A. Project management

  B. Leadership

  C. Negotiation

  D. Problem solving

☑ **B.** Leadership involves the ability to guide, motivate, and direct a team.

☒ **A, C,** and **D** are incorrect. **A** is incorrect because project management is not a skill—it is a methodology. **C** and **D** are incorrect because they both represent essential capabilities that are part of leadership.

20. A project manager who is participating in training, continuing education, and development is demonstrating which aspect of project management?

 A. Knowledge transfer and integration

 B. Training future project managers

 C. Learning business analysis techniques

 D. Collecting the right number of PDUs in a one-year cycle

 ☑ **A.** Continuing knowledge transfer is important for a project manager. Participating in training, continuing education, and development in the project management profession, related professions, or other professions demonstrates the ongoing need to maintain project management expertise.

 ☒ **B, C,** and **D** are incorrect. **B** is incorrect because training future managers is not the main focus of a project manager. **C** is incorrect because the question does not relate to business analysis. **D** is incorrect because the question does not pertain to the PMI requirement to maintain 60 professional development units (PDUs) in a three-year cycle.

21. Which of the following skill sets does a project manager demonstrate when exhibiting knowledge of and expertise in the industry and the organization with a focus on better outcomes?

 A. Technical project management

 B. Generic project management

 C. Leadership and research

 D. Strategic and business management

 ☑ **D.** Knowledge of and expertise in the industry and the organization with a focus on better outcomes demonstrates strategic and business management.

 ☒ **A, B,** and **C** are incorrect. **A** is incorrect because technical project management is the knowledge, skills, and behaviors related to specific business domains. **B** is incorrect because generic project management focuses internally, not strategically. **C** is incorrect because while leadership is a key skill for a project manager, research is not.

Project Integration Management

In this chapter, you will

- Understand the seven project management processes in the project integration management knowledge area
- Identify the input, tools, techniques and outputs defined in the seven processes in project integration management
- Understand the purpose of project integration management and the project manager's role within it
- Identify concepts and procedures related to project change management
- Identify tailoring consideration in project integration management and recognize key documents
- Identify methods for project integration and knowledge management

The Project Integration Management knowledge area accounts for 9 percent (27) of the questions on the CAPM exam. The *PMBOK Guide, Sixth Edition*, Sections 4.1 through 4.7, cover the seven tasks in the Project Integration Management knowledge area.

Project Integration Management recognizes that no part of the profession of project management acts in isolation, and in fact there is a high degree of interdependency between various parts of the profession of project management. As such, a lot of the information discussed in this chapter reaches across many other knowledge areas within the profession. In addition to recognizing the interdependency of all other knowledge areas, Project Integration Management also specifically addresses those activities, such as change control processes, which are carried out over more than one knowledge area.

The 27 practice questions in this chapter are mapped to the style and frequency of question types you will see on the CAPM exam.

1. Which of the following activities would you undertake as a project manager to best understand the project environment?

    A. Schedule and all resources

    B. Cultural and social issues

    C. Project budget approval process

    D. Detailed requirements analysis

2. Which of the following is a best practice to maximize the chances of project success?

    A. Calculate the project timeline and initial budget.

    B. Recruit the key project skills as early as possible.

    C. Develop the project charter and scope of work.

    D. Write a comprehensive change control process.

3. Which project document should you look at to ensure that you have the authority needed to carry out your project manager roles and responsibilities?

    A. Work breakdown structure

    B. Project charter

    C. Requirements document

    D. Project schedule

4. To complete the project charter, which of the following should be in place?

    A. The detailed features list to be delivered

    B. The not-to-exceed price for the project

    C. The agreed-upon contract for the project

    D. The estimated labor costs of the project

5. Who provides you with a statement of work (SOW)?

    A. The end-user group

    B. Your line manager

    C. The project director

    D. The project sponsor

6. When writing the project charter, which of the following would be least likely to help you clarify the influences on the project?

    A. Existing skills and knowledge within the organization

    B. Regulatory standards that are about to be approved

    C. The infrastructure in place to support an IT solution

    D. The likely political changes in local government

7. What do you do if the project charter you have developed has not yet been approved by the project sponsor?

   A. Start interviewing potential team members in anticipation of project approval.

   B. Start working on the project plan as a work in progress.

   C. State the likely impact of proceeding without approval.

   D. Negotiate a compromise with the line manager that considers the next project.

8. Which of the following tools and techniques would best help you proceed with the project chartering process?

   A. Matrix management structure

   B. Available project templates

   C. Lessons learned

   D. Expert judgment of others

9. Which of the following is essential for the project charter to be approved?

   A. Detailed work and schedule estimates

   B. A list of all the resources required

   C. The business need for the project

   D. A list of all the risks in the project

10. What is the document called that contains the market demand and cost–benefit analysis that justifies the go-ahead for the project?

    A. Contract

    B. Statement of work

    C. Business case

    D. Organizational asset

11. To ensure that you take a comprehensive approach to identifying stakeholders, you decide to seek the expert judgment of this stakeholder:

    A. Database architect

    B. Resource allocation manager

    C. Competitors

    D. Project sponsor

12. For a project, which deliverable should be created after the project statement of work?

    A. Scope statement

    B. Management plan

    C. Charter

    D. Requirements document

13. What document formally authorizes a project?

    A. Business case

    B. Project charter

    C. Project statement of work (SOW)

    D. Project management plan

14. Select the process that assigns the project manager to a project.

    A. Develop Project Charter

    B. Develop Project Management Plan

    C. Develop Business Case

    D. Develop Strategic Plan

15. Which two knowledge areas are involved in the Initiating process group?

    A. Project Integration Management and Project Scope Management

    B. Project Scope Management and Project Schedule Management

    C. Project Integration Management and Project Stakeholder Management

    D. Project Scope Management and Project Risk Management

16. You have identified specific resource requirements in your project charter. What is this called?

    A. An estimate of the resources required for the various project phases

    B. A preassignment section on why the project is dependent upon the expertise of persons

    C. A RACI chart showing all project resources

    D. A RACI chart that includes roles and responsibilities of your project's stakeholders

17. You are a project manager carrying out the first adaptive project for the company. For each iteration, you will need to ensure your team carries out all of the following except:

    A. Collect Requirements

    B. Define Scope

    C. Create WBS

    D. Develop Project Charter

18. Which of the following are documents that are generally originated outside of the project and are used as input to the project?

    A. Business requirements document

    B. Business documents

    C. Stakeholder requirements document

    D. Project change control process

19. What two things does a project charter link together?

    A. The sponsor and the project manager

    B. The objectives and the timeline

    C. The project and the strategic objectives of the company

    D. The funding and the deliverables

20. What two outputs are created in the Develop Project Charter process?

    A. Project charter and constraint list

    B. Project charter and business documents

    C. Project charter and organizational process assets

    D. Project charter and assumption log

21. For each project, you use a template to create a customized communications management plan and stakeholder engagement plan. These are both examples of documents:

    A. Provided by the sponsor for the project

    B. Created by the business analyst during the initiation phase

    C. That are components of a project management plan

    D. Created as a part of the Initiating process group

22. What document contains a set of approvals for the project requirements?

    A. Business case

    B. Solution requirements

    C. Project charter

    D. Feasibility study

23. Which of the following best describes the main purpose of the project management plan?

    A. To initiate and approve the project

    B. To define both project and product scope

    C. To describe how the project will be executed, monitored, and controlled

    D. To assess which projects should be done

24. Which project change requests must go through the approved change control process?

    A. Only those that have an impact on project scope

    B. Any change request that affects scope, time, cost, or quality

    C. Only those change requests that the project manager decides should go through the process

    D. All change requests must go through the change control process

25. What is the name of the group of people responsible for reviewing, evaluating, and deciding on changes to the project?

   A. Change control board

   B. Project steering group

   C. Project team

   D. Stakeholders

26. Consulting stakeholders and project team members and using your own knowledge are all examples of what sort of tool or technique used in the Project Integration Management knowledge area?

   A. Stakeholder engagement

   B. Meetings

   C. Expert judgment

   D. Analytical techniques

27. What is the correct order of project activities?

   A. Develop project management plan, execute project, develop project charter, conduct project selection

   B. Conduct project selection, develop project charter, execute project, develop project management plan

   C. Conduct project selection, develop project charter, develop project management plan, execute project

   D. Develop project charter, develop project management plan, execute project, conduct project selection

1. B	**10.** C	**19.** C
2. C	**11.** D	**20.** D
3. B	**12.** C	**21.** C
4. C	**13.** B	**22.** C
5. D	**14.** A	**23.** C
6. D	**15.** C	**24.** D
7. C	**16.** B	**25.** A
8. D	**17.** D	**26.** C
9. C	**18.** B	**27.** C

1. Which of the following activities would you undertake as a project manager to best understand the project environment?

   A. Schedule and all resources

   B. Cultural and social issues

   C. Project budget approval process

   D. Detailed requirements analysis

   ☑ **B.** When planning and implementing a project, one of the considerations is the project environment, including the cultural and social issues that may affect the success of the project.

   ☒ **A, C,** and **D** are incorrect. **A** and **C** are incorrect because they are specific to the workings of the project rather than to the environment the project exists within. **D** is incorrect because requirements are details evaluated later in the planning processes.

2. Which of the following is a best practice to maximize the chances of project success?

   A. Calculate the project timeline and initial budget.

   B. Recruit the key project skills as early as possible.

   C. Develop the project charter and scope of work.

   D. Write a comprehensive change control process.

   ☑ **C.** A project charter with a well-defined scope of work is necessary to calculating timelines, calculating budgets, recruiting skills, and creating a change management process. The development of the project charter is part of the initiation phase.

   ☒ **A, B,** and **D** are incorrect. They are part of scope control and detailed planning, which follow project charter creation. **A** is incorrect because a project timeline and budget cannot be created without knowing what is in scope for the project. **B** is incorrect and should be undertaken as early as possible, but skills cannot be determined until the scope of the effort is determined. **D** is incorrect because the timing for a change control process is after an understanding of the scope of the effort is complete.

3. Which project document should you look at to ensure that you have the authority needed to carry out your project manager roles and responsibilities?

   A. Work breakdown structure

   B. Project charter

   C. Requirements document

   D. Project schedule

   ☑ **B.** The project charter is the document that formally authorizes a project and gives the project manager the authority to apply organizational resources to project activities. A project manager is identified and assigned as early in the project as is feasible. The project manager should always be assigned prior to the start of planning, and preferably while the project charter is being developed. Without an approved charter, the project manager has no authority within the organization.

☒ **A**, **C**, and **D** are incorrect. **A** and **D** are incorrect because they are a part of the project plan, which follows from a project's charter. The work breakdown structure (WBS) itemizes the work to be done in the project. The project schedule aligns the work to be done with a calendar for completion. **C** is incorrect because a requirements document is created as a part of the Execution phase and details the product that will be created by the project charter.

4. To complete the project charter, which of the following should be in place?

   A. The detailed features list to be delivered

   B. The not-to-exceed price for the project

   C. The agreed-upon contract for the project

   D. The estimated labor costs of the project

   ☑ **C.** The project charter inputs may include the contract if the project is being done for an external customer. The other options are all subsets of an agreed-upon contract or calculations that lead to an agreed-upon contract.

   ☒ **A**, **B**, and **D** are incorrect. **A** is incorrect because only a high-level list of features is created at the project charter point. **B** is incorrect because the not-to-exceed detail may be a component of the contract with the external organization; however, not all contracts have a not-to-exceed component. **D** is incorrect because although labor costs may have been estimated to arrive at pricing, those costs would be a variable used in calculating the contract price.

5. Who provides you with a statement of work (SOW)?

   A. The end-user group

   B. Your line manager

   C. The project director

   D. The project sponsor

   ☑ **D.** The project statement of work (SOW) is provided by the project initiator or sponsor for internal projects based on a business need, product, or service requirement.

   ☒ **A**, **B**, and **C** are incorrect. **A** is incorrect because the end-user group represents the stakeholders who will ultimately use the product of the project on an ongoing basis; this group may have input to the product that is needed but would not provide the final statement of work. **B** is incorrect as it implies a matrix management organization, and in that situation the line manager is responsible for your career, not your project. **C** is incorrect because there is no project role called "project director" (in the financial industry there are often managing directors, but those still are not project managers).

6. When writing the project charter, which of the following would be least likely to help you clarify the influences on the project?

    A. Existing skills and knowledge within the organization

    B. Regulatory standards that are about to be approved

    C. The infrastructure in place to support an IT solution

    D. The likely political changes in local government

    ☑ **D.** As a project manager, you must consider many factors when developing a project charter; however, external political changes will have the least impact on an internal software solution being developed by your own company.

    ☒ **A**, **B**, and **C** are incorrect. **A** is incorrect because it is important to know the existing skills and knowledge within the organization when resourcing the project and that will be dealt with after the project charter is written and hopefully approved. **B** is incorrect because both existing and pending regulatory changes can directly influence the scope and efforts of the project. **C** is incorrect because the existing infrastructure in use by IT is extremely important, given that the solution will be developed in-house.

7. What do you do if the project charter you have developed has not yet been approved by the project sponsor?

    A. Start interviewing potential team members in anticipation of project approval.

    B. Start working on the project plan as a work in progress.

    C. State the likely impact of proceeding without approval.

    D. Negotiate a compromise with the line manager that considers the next project.

    ☑ **C.** As a project manager you must not start a project without an approved charter. If the project starts without approval, organizational resources may be misdirected or wasted and rework may be created. Your authority to proceed should be given by the ultimate authority: the project sponsor.

    ☒ **A**, **B**, and **D** are incorrect. **A** is incorrect, as it would let people know about a project that has not yet been authorized, and in the world of dealing with the emotions of team members, it might get someone's hopes up falsely. **B** is incorrect because a project plan follows a project charter; the project plan requires the authority to manage the project, and said authority has not yet been acquired. **D** is incorrect, although an interesting answer—recall that the line manager's job and your project manager's job have two different goals and you need to be true to the goal of the project.

8. Which of the following tools and techniques would best help you proceed with the project chartering process?

    A. Matrix management structure

    B. Available project templates

    C. Lessons learned

    D. Expert judgment of others

☑ **D.** When developing a project charter, the input of expert judgment often is used to help identify the inputs that must be considered in this process.

☒ **A, B**, and **C** are incorrect. **A** is incorrect because a matrix management structure involves the line or direct managers, who would not have knowledge of the inputs needed for your project. **B** is incorrect because this may be helpful, but templates in and of themselves are skeletons of documents without specific reference to inputs you may need. **C** is incorrect because lessons learned do come from prior projects, but asking experts should come first.

9. Which of the following is essential for the project charter to be approved?

   A. Detailed work and schedule estimates

   B. A list of all the resources required

   C. The business need for the project

   D. A list of all the risks in the project

   ☑ **C.** The business need for the project is an essential input to the project charter. The detailed estimates and lists of risks are produced as part of project planning, which comes after the project chartering process. Some general and top-level resources are included in the project charter, but not all the resources for the project.

   ☒ **A, B**, and **D** are incorrect. **A** is incorrect because detailed work and schedule estimates are developed during the planning phase of a project. **B** is incorrect because the detailed resources required will not be known until the full set of requirements is developed. **D** is incorrect because of the word *all*. Risks are important, but the only risks identified at the Develop Project Charter process are high-level risks—product risks come later.

10. What is the document called that contains the market demand and cost–benefit analysis that justifies the go-ahead for the project?

    A. Contract

    B. Statement of work

    C. Business case

    D. Organizational asset

    ☑ **C.** The business case contains the business need and cost–benefit analysis that justify the go-ahead of the project; it is created because of market demand, organizational need, customer request, technological advance, or legal requirement. All other options are inputs to the process of developing a project charter.

    ☒ **A, B**, and **D** are incorrect. **A** is incorrect because a contract implies an external entity involved with your own company; therefore, a contract would not contain cost–benefit information. **B** is incorrect because a statement of work (SOW) identifies all the deliverables for the project without regard for cost–benefit analysis. **D** is incorrect because an organizational process asset references the templates for documents used within an organization and may include policies and process references as well.

11. To ensure that you take a comprehensive approach to identifying stakeholders, you decide to seek the expert judgment of this stakeholder:

A. Database architect

B. Resource allocation manager

C. Competitors

D. Project sponsor

☑ **D.** As part of stakeholder analysis, groups or individuals, such as senior management, project sponsor, project team, industry groups, and even technical or professional associations, should contribute to the process.

☒ **A, B,** and **C** are incorrect. **A** is incorrect because the database architect may not be a member of the project team. **B** is incorrect because the resource allocation manager's job is to supply project resources as they are needed. **C** is incorrect because competitors are not a source of identifying stakeholders for an internal project, though they may be a stakeholder group that should be analyzed during the project.

12. For a project, which deliverable should be created after the project statement of work?

A. Scope statement

B. Management plan

C. Charter

D. Requirements document

☑ **C.** With the business need identified and high-level deliverables defined in the statement of work (SOW), the project charter is created next to give the project manager the authority to work on the project and create the product deliverables.

☒ **A, B,** and **D** are incorrect. Each is an output of the planning phase, which follows the initiation phase. If the project charter does not exist, the project manager has no mandate to create the scope statement, management plan, or requirements document.

13. What document formally authorizes a project?

A. Business case

B. Project charter

C. Project statement of work (SOW)

D. Project management plan

☑ **B.** The Develop Project Charter process assigns the project manager and produces the project charter that officially authorizes the project.

☒ **A, C,** and **D** are incorrect. **A** is incorrect because the business case explains the need for the project. **C** is incorrect because the SOW, part of the agreements, is a written description of the project's product, service, or result. The business case and agreements serve as inputs to the Develop Project Charter process. **D** is incorrect because the project management plan is developed after the project charter is approved and the project manager is assigned.

14. Select the process that assigns the project manager to a project.

    A. Develop Project Charter

    B. Develop Project Management Plan

    C. Develop Business Case

    D. Develop Strategic Plan

    ☑ **A.** The Develop Project Charter process assigns the project manager and produces the project charter that authorizes the project and links the need for the project to the organization's strategic plan.

    ☒ **B, C,** and **D** are incorrect. **B** is incorrect because the project management plan is created by the project manager in the planning phase. **C** is incorrect because it is a made-up process name; the business case provides the strategic and financial justification for the project and therefore precedes the project charter. **D** is incorrect because it is a made-up process name; the strategic plan precedes the project charter.

15. Which two knowledge areas are involved in the Initiating process group?

    A. Project Integration Management and Project Scope Management

    B. Project Scope Management and Project Schedule Management

    C. Project Integration Management and Project Stakeholder Management

    D. Project Scope Management and Project Risk Management

    ☑ **C.** The knowledge area Project Integration Management contains the Develop Project Charter process, and the Project Stakeholder Management process contains Identify Stakeholders.

    ☒ **A, B,** and **D** are incorrect. **A** is incorrect because Project Scope Management has no processes in the Initiating process group. **B** is incorrect because neither Project Scope Management nor Project Schedule Management have processes in the Initiating process group. **D** is incorrect because Project Risk Management has no processes in the Initiating process group.

16. You have identified specific resource requirements in your project charter. What is this called?

    A. An estimate of the resources required for the various project phases

    B. A preassignment section on why the project is dependent upon the expertise of persons

    C. A RACI chart showing all project resources

    D. A RACI chart that includes roles and responsibilities of your project's stakeholders

    ☑ **B.** When physical or team resources for a project are determined in advance, they are considered preassigned.

    ☒ **A, C,** and **D** are incorrect. **A** is incorrect because estimating resources required for the various project phases is done in the Planning process group. **C** and **D** are incorrect because the RACI chart is a useful tool to use to ensure clear assignment of roles and responsibilities when the team consists of internal and external resources.

17. You are a project manager carrying out the first adaptive project for the company. For each iteration, you will need to ensure your team carries out all of the following except:

A. Collect Requirements

B. Define Scope

C. Create WBS

D. Develop Project Charter

☑ **D**. A project charter would be created one time, at the beginning of the first iteration. In each successive iteration, small working products would be delivered through the cycle of collecting requirements, defining the scope of what will be worked on within the next iteration, and creating a work breakdown structure of tasks and deliverables in the iteration.

☒ **A**, **B**, and **C** are incorrect. **A** is incorrect because an iteration in an adaptive project is driven by the requirements, fine-tuning a small set of requirements, and creating a working product for those requirements. **B** is incorrect because defining the scope of what will and will not be done in each iteration is crucial to the success of the iteration. **C** is incorrect because understanding the tasks of what must be done in each iteration defines who will be needed to accomplish the tasks, thus making this an essential step.

18. Which of the following are documents that are generally originated outside of the project and are used as input to the project?

A. Business requirements document

B. Business documents

C. Stakeholder requirements document

D. Project change control process

☑ **B**. Business documents are provided by the sponsor as an input to the Develop Project Charter process.

☒ **A**, **C**, and **D** are incorrect. **A** is incorrect because the business requirements document may be developed within the project as a part of the project charter. **C** is incorrect because stakeholder requirements are documented within the Collect Requirements process. **D** is incorrect because a project's change control process is decided after the project charter is complete.

19. What two things does a project charter link together?

A. The sponsor and the project manager

B. The objectives and the timeline

C. The project and the strategic objectives of the company

D. The funding and the deliverables

☑ **C.** Each project is undertaken for the benefit of the company, and the charter brings together the "why" of the project with how it aligns to strategic goals.

☒ **A**, **B**, and **D** are incorrect. **A** is incorrect because a project manager is given authority in the project charter; the manager may change, but the charter doesn't have to simultaneously change. **B** is incorrect because the timeline is not set in the project charter. **D** is incorrect because the funding and deliverables are both identified in the charter, but funding is not a fixed amount for most projects.

20. What two outputs are created in the Develop Project Charter process?

   A. Project charter and constraint list

   B. Project charter and business documents

   C. Project charter and organizational process assets

   D. Project charter and assumption log

   ☑ **D.** The assumptions about a project are created together with the project charter.

   ☒ **A**, **B**, and **C** are incorrect. **A** is incorrect because a constraint list is not created as an output of the Develop Project Charter process. **B** is incorrect because business documents are an input to the Develop Project Charter process. **C** is incorrect because organizational process assets preexist a project charter.

21. For each project, you use a template to create a customized communications management plan and stakeholder engagement plan. These are both examples of documents:

   A. Provided by the sponsor for the project

   B. Created by the business analyst during the initiation phase

   C. That are components of a project management plan

   D. Created as a part of the Initiating process group

   ☑ **C.** A communications plan and a stakeholder engagement plan are part of a project management plan.

   ☒ **A**, **B**, and **D** are incorrect. **A** is incorrect because the sponsor does not provide these documents; rather, they are created within the project. **B** is incorrect because these documents are created in the planning phase. **D** is incorrect because these documents are created as a part of the planning phase.

22. What document contains a set of approvals for the project requirements?

   A. Business case

   B. Solution requirements

   C. Project charter

   D. Feasibility study

   ☑ **C.** A project charter contains the high-level product characteristics and is a signed-off, approved document.

⊠ **A**, **B**, and **D** are incorrect. **A** is incorrect because a business case does not contain project requirements; rather, it presents a business problem and ways to solve it. **B** is incorrect because solution requirements are developed during the collect requirements process and contain lower-level product details. **D** is incorrect because the feasibility study would precede the project.

23. Which of the following best describes the main purpose of the project management plan?

  A. To initiate and approve the project

  B. To define both project and product scope

  C. To describe how the project will be executed, monitored, and controlled

  D. To assess which projects should be done

  ☑ **C.** The project management plan describes how the rest of the project will be executed, monitored, and controlled and closed.

  ⊠ **A**, **B**, and **D** are incorrect. **A** is incorrect because the project charter initiates and approves the project. **B** is incorrect: the scope statement defines both project and product scope. **D** is incorrect: the business case can be used to assess which projects should be done.

24. Which project change requests must go through the approved change control process?

  A. Only those that have an impact on project scope

  B. Any change request that affects scope, time, cost, or quality

  C. Only those change requests that the project manager decides should go through the process

  D. All change requests must go through the change control process

  ☑ **D.** All change requests must be considered as per the approved change control process.

  ⊠ **A**, **B**, and **C** are incorrect. **A** is incorrect because all change requests, not just those that affect project scope, must go through the defined change control process. **B** is incorrect because all change requests, not just those that affect scope, time, quality, and cost, must go through the defined change control process. **C** is incorrect because the project manager does play a proactive part in influencing those factors that may lead to change requests being initiated, but once initiated the requests must all go through the approved change control process.

25. What is the name of the group of people responsible for reviewing, evaluating, and deciding on changes to the project?

  A. Change control board

  B. Project steering group

  C. Project team

  D. Stakeholders

☑ **A.** The change control board is responsible for reviewing, evaluating, and deciding on changes to the project.

☒ **B, C,** and **D** are incorrect. **B** is incorrect because the project steering group is responsible for providing senior-level advice, oversight, and project governance. **C** is incorrect because the project team is responsible for carrying out the project work under the guidance of the project manager. **D** is incorrect because stakeholders have many roles within the project, and members of the change control board are certainly stakeholders, but the broadest definition includes everyone who can affect or be affected by the project.

26. Consulting stakeholders and project team members and using your own knowledge are all examples of what sort of tool or technique used in the Project Integration Management knowledge area?

    A. Stakeholder engagement

    B. Meetings

    C. Expert judgment

    D. Analytical techniques

☑ **C.** The description in the question refers to different categories of experts who may be consulted for their advice and opinion.

☒ **A, B,** and **D** are incorrect. **A** is incorrect because stakeholder engagement is the activity carried out as the focus of the Project Stakeholder Management knowledge area. **B** is incorrect because meetings are used to gather groups of stakeholders together to discuss and make decisions. **D** is incorrect because analytical techniques are mathematical techniques used to interpret raw data.

27. What is the correct order of project activities?

    A. Develop project management plan, execute project, develop project charter, conduct project selection

    B. Conduct project selection, develop project charter, execute project, develop project management plan

    C. Conduct project selection, develop project charter, develop project management plan, execute project

    D. Develop project charter, develop project management plan, execute project, conduct project selection

☑ **C.** Project selection feeds into the project charter, which in turn feeds into the development of the project management plan. The project management plan is used as the basis for project execution.

☒ **A, B,** and **D** are incorrect. **A** is incorrect because project selection and development of the project charter must be carried out before the development of the project management plan. **B** is incorrect because the development of the project management plan must occur before execution of the work. **D** is incorrect because conducting project selection must be done first in the process.

5

Project Scope Management

In this chapter, you will

- Understand the six project management processes in the Project Scope Management knowledge area
- Identify the inputs, tools, techniques, and outputs defined in the six processes in project scope management
- Identify key concepts and tailoring consideration for project scope management, as well as the key roles
- Identify the purpose and elements of a work breakdown structure (WBS) for both product and project scope
- Understand project scope management for agile/adaptive projects, including the use of prototypes

Project scope encompasses the entirety of all work that needs to be done in a project to bring the deliverables of the project to life. The Project Scope Management process group is responsible for identifying all the work the project team must accomplish in order for the project to be successful. It is in this process group that the requirements are created. Certified Associate in Project Management (CAPM) candidates are tested on five objectives that demonstrate the candidate's understanding of the concept of scope creation, scope change, and scope modification during the project.

The 27 practice questions in this chapter are mapped to the style and frequency of question types you will see on the CAPM exam.

1. Which document establishes a collective understanding of the project among the project stakeholders and can assist you in managing stakeholder expectations?

   A. Stakeholder management plan

   B. Project scope statement

   C. Scope management plan

   D. Program charter

2. If you are in the process of defining and controlling what is, and what is not, included in the project, what process are you performing?

   A. Project documentation management

   B. Project change control

   C. Plan scope management

   D. Formal acceptance documents

3. Which statement *best* describes the scope management plan?

   A. The scope management plan provides guidance on how project scope will be defined, documented, verified, managed, and controlled.

   B. The scope management plan documents how requirements will be analyzed, documented, and managed throughout the project.

   C. The scope management plan describes in detail the project's deliverables and the work required to create those deliverables.

   D. The scope management plan is a deliverable-oriented hierarchical decomposition of the work to be executed by the project team.

4. As you develop the project scope statement as the foundation for work your company is performing, you should:

   A. Ask the project team to list the major project milestones

   B. Identify any new job seekers for open positions

   C. Use the resource traceability matrix in your data analysis

   D. Include acceptance criteria to use as closure guidelines

5. Your contracted project is running behind schedule, is over budget, and is failing to deliver the features originally promised. As the project manager, you hold a team meeting to reinforce with all project members that all work between now and the completion of the project must focus on a prioritized list of activities. What best defines this list of activities?

   A. Shortest-duration tasks

   B. Requirements documentation

   C. Critical-path tasks

   D. Lowest-cost tasks

6. Which of the following is the process of formalizing acceptance of the project's completed deliverables?

    A. Control Scope

    B. Define Scope

    C. Validate Scope

    D. Verify Deliverables

7. Which statement describes the purpose of the requirements traceability matrix?

    A. It describes in detail the project's deliverables and the work required to create those deliverables and includes product and project scope description.

    B. It ensures that requirements approved in the requirements documentation are delivered at the end of the project and helps manage changes to product scope.

    C. It is a narrative description of products or services to be delivered by the project and is received from the customer for external projects.

    D. It provides the necessary information from a business standpoint to determine whether the project is worth the required investment.

8. Which of the following would you use to help clarify technical details that you were not familiar with and their impact on the project scope?

    A. Experienced managers

    B. Special interest groups

    C. Expert judgment

    D. Similar project plans

9. Your current project has produced a requirements management plan. What is the purpose of this document?

    A. The requirements management plan links requirements to their origin and traces them throughout the project.

    B. The requirements management plan documents how requirements will be analyzed, documented, and managed throughout the project.

    C. The requirements management plan describes how individual requirements meet the business need for the project.

    D. The requirements management plan provides guidance on how project scope will be defined, documented, verified, managed, and controlled.

10. Which three Project Scope Management processes use the project charter as an input?

    A. Plan Scope Management, Create WBS, and Validate Scope

    B. Create WBS, Validate Scope, and Control Scope

    C. Control Scope, Define Scope, and Collect Requirements

    D. Plan Scope Management, Collect Requirements, and Define Scope

11. Which Project Scope Management process uses only data analysis as a tool and technique?

   A. Plan Scope Management

   B. Collect Requirements

   C. Define Scope

   D. Control Scope

12. Which Project Scope Management process creates the scope baseline?

   A. Plan Scope Management

   B. Control Scope

   C. Create WBS

   D. Validate Scope

13. Your current project has multiple stakeholders representing each of the departments. In this case, who would approve the scope statement that you develop?

   A. The project team members

   B. The project sponsor

   C. The project manager

   D. The financial manager

14. What action should the project manager take when finding out the organization lacks a formal requirements management process that can accommodate the current project?

   A. Pause the project and create a formal requirements management process.

   B. Tailor the way the Project Scope Management processes are applied.

   C. Purchase a commercial off-the-shelf requirements management tool.

   D. Add requirements to the SharePoint repository as an alternative.

15. What is the project manager tailoring if he or she is deciding to use an adaptive, predictive, or hybrid approach?

   A. Validation and control approach

   B. Governance approach

   C. Procurement approach

   D. Development approach

16. Which of the following can help unstable requirements move to the point of being stable and well defined?

   A. Lean techniques

   B. RACI chart

   C. Project management plan

   D. Root-cause analysis

17. When examining the validation and control mechanisms in place for the current project, what should a project manager be looking to tailor if appropriate for the project?

    A. Governance approaches

    B. Control-related policies, procedures, and guidelines

    C. Change control for requirements

    D. Matrix management

18. Which of the following is considered a primary purpose of a project's WBS?

    A. Clarify the responsibility for project tasks.

    B. Communicate with all stakeholders.

    C. Define the business need for the project.

    D. Detail the dates for the work packages.

19. Project management office support deliverables should be considered which of the following in the WBS?

    A. Top-level milestone

    B. External deliverable

    C. Work package

    D. Project management artifact

20. Your project requires that you hire multiple third-party vendors, and you are considering elements to include in the procurement management plan for the project. Before completing the procurement management plan, you should first:

    A. Review project assets on procurement

    B. Develop activity cost estimates

    C. Prepare a prequalified seller list

    D. Review the WBS

21. What does the 100 percent rule refer to?

    A. The ratio of requirements that need to be implemented for the project to be a success

    B. The sum of quality tasks in a project together with the administrative tasks

    C. The presence of all product and project work in the WBS with nothing left out and no extra work included

    D. The ratio of stakeholder engagement required for the project to move to the Executing phase

22. Which of the following is a generally accepted business practice used in creating a project's WBS?

    A. Structure it so product scope and project scope are easily managed.

    B. Set it up to show the complete scope of the work to be carried out on the project.

    C. Use it to define the management control points for each of the major deliverables.

    D. Define the solution to the problem in terms of a product, service, or result.

23. Your team has chosen a user story to prototype for an area of high risk in the project. Which of the following *best* describes the process in which you are involved?

    A. Calculating the total duration of the project from the start

    B. Counting the total number of work packages in the project

    C. Allocating responsibilities for the project work to individuals in the team

    D. Subdividing the project work into smaller, more manageable components

24. In an agile project, who decides who will perform the work for the next period's defined scope?

    A. Product owner

    B. Project manager

    C. Scrum Master

    D. Team members

25. Which of the following allows agile teams to see what they've accomplished and shows changes in scope during an iteration?

    A. Product backlog

    B. Burnup chart

    C. RACI chart

    D. Control chart

26. In developing project scope, one approach is to:

    A. Describe scope in user stories

    B. Determine scope through high-level infrastructure

    C. Use the project's budget to set a financial baseline

    D. Include nonfunctional requirements for products, services, or results

27. You have made the decision to control risk through planning on your current project and therefore conclude that your scope management approach should be:

    A. Predictive

    B. Adaptive

    C. Iterative

    D. Lean

1. B	**10.** D	**19.** C
2. C	**11.** D	**20.** D
3. A	**12.** C	**21.** C
4. D	**13.** B	**22.** B
5. B	**14.** B	**23.** D
6. C	**15.** D	**24.** D
7. B	**16.** A	**25.** B
8. C	**17.** B	**26.** A
9. B	**18.** B	**27.** A

1. Which document establishes a collective understanding of the project among the project stakeholders and can assist you in managing stakeholder expectations?

   A. Stakeholder management plan

   B. Project scope statement

   C. Scope management plan

   D. Program charter

   ☑ **B.** The PM ensures that the context and framework of the project are properly defined, assessed, and documented in the form of a project scope statement. Project stakeholders should verify and approve the project scope statement.

   ☒ **A, C,** and **D** are incorrect. **A** is incorrect because the stakeholder management plan has been replaced with the stakeholder engagement plan. **C** is incorrect because the scope management plan is an input to defining the scope, which produces the project scope statement. **D** is incorrect because the project charter ensures a mutual understanding of deliverables and milestones.

2. If you are in the process of defining and controlling what is, and what is not, included in the project, what process are you performing?

   A. Project documentation management

   B. Project change control

   C. Plan scope management

   D. Formal acceptance documents

   ☑ **C.** The Plan Scope Management process defines and controls what is, and what is not, included in the project.

   ☒ **A, B,** and **D** are incorrect. **A** and **B** are incorrect because project documentation management and project change control are procedures to allow the control of changes to scope only. **D** is incorrect because formal acceptance documents are part of the Close Project or Phase process.

3. Which statement *best* describes the scope management plan?

   A. The scope management plan provides guidance on how project scope will be defined, documented, verified, managed, and controlled.

   B. The scope management plan documents how requirements will be analyzed, documented, and managed throughout the project.

   C. The scope management plan describes in detail the project's deliverables and the work required to create those deliverables.

   D. The scope management plan is a deliverable-oriented hierarchical decomposition of the work to be executed by the project team.

☑ **A.** The scope management plan provides guidance on how project scope will be defined, documented, verified, managed, and controlled. It may be formal or informal, highly detailed or broadly framed, based on the project needs.

☒ **B, C,** and **D** are incorrect. **B** is incorrect because detailed requirements are not part of a project charter. **C** is incorrect because it describes the project scope statement. **D** is incorrect because it describes the WBS.

4. As you develop the project scope statement as the foundation for work your company is performing, you should:

   A. Ask the project team to list the major project milestones

   B. Identify any new job seekers for open positions

   C. Use the resource traceability matrix in your data analysis

   D. Include acceptance criteria to use as closure guidelines

   ☑ **D.** Acceptance criteria are documented in the project scope statement. Acceptance criteria are also considered an important part of contractual agreements on external projects and used as project closure guidelines.

   ☒ **A, B,** and **C** are incorrect. **A** is incorrect because major deliverables are sometimes tied to major milestones and are displayed in a milestone chart, which is an output of developing the schedule. **B** is incorrect because new team members are added as part of acquiring the project team. **C** is incorrect because resource traceability matrix is a made-up term. A responsibility assignment matrix shows the project resources assigned to each work package.

5. Your contracted project is running behind schedule, is over budget, and is failing to deliver the features originally promised. As the project manager, you hold a team meeting to reinforce with all project members that all work between now and the completion of the project must focus on a prioritized list of activities. What best defines this list of activities?

   A. Shortest-duration tasks

   B. Requirements documentation

   C. Critical-path tasks

   D. Lowest-cost tasks

   ☑ **B.** The requirements documentation helps define the priorities of the requirements as part of the Collect Requirements process. This is where the project team determines how resources can be best used to obtain contract acceptance.

   ☒ **A, C,** and **D** are incorrect. **A** is incorrect because shortest-duration tasks will give an impression of progress, but that focus may be on the wrong tasks. **C** is incorrect because focusing on critical-path tasks will preserve or shorten the duration but may not ensure meeting the overall contract. **D** is incorrect because focusing on lowest-cost tasks will help short-term cash flow but may not meet the contract or stakeholders' expectations.

6. Which of the following is the process of formalizing acceptance of the project's completed deliverables?

   A. Control Scope

   B. Define Scope

   C. Validate Scope

   D. Verify Deliverables

   ☑ **C.** The Validate Scope process formalizes acceptance of completed project deliverables using verified deliverables from the Control Quality process as an input.

   ☒ **A, B,** and **D** are incorrect. **A** is incorrect because Control Scope is about monitoring the status of the project and product scope, not getting the deliverables accepted. **B** is incorrect because Define Scope is done early in the project to create a detailed description of the project. **D** is incorrect because Verified Deliverables is not a process; rather, it is an output from the Control Quality process used as an input to Validate Scope.

7. Which statement describes the purpose of the requirements traceability matrix?

   A. It describes in detail the project's deliverables and the work required to create those deliverables and includes product and project scope description.

   B. It ensures that requirements approved in the requirements documentation are delivered at the end of the project and helps manage changes to product scope.

   C. It is a narrative description of products or services to be delivered by the project and is received from the customer for external projects.

   D. It provides the necessary information from a business standpoint to determine whether the project is worth the required investment.

   ☑ **B.** The requirements traceability matrix ensures that requirements approved in the requirements documentation are delivered at the end of the project. The requirements traceability matrix also provides a structure for managing change to product scope.

   ☒ **A, C,** and **D** are incorrect. **A** describes the project scope statement. **C** is the project statement of work used in developing the project charter. **D** describes the project business case.

8. Which of the following would you use to help clarify technical details that you were not familiar with and their impact on the project scope?

   A. Experienced managers

   B. Special interest groups

   C. Expert judgment

   D. Similar project plans

☑ **C.** The use of expert judgment is recommended when a project manager comes across an area that is unfamiliar.

☒ **A**, **B**, and **D** are incorrect. **A** is incorrect because "experienced managers" is ambiguous, as you cannot tell if they are business managers, secretarial managers, quality managers, etc. **B** and **D** are incorrect because special interest groups (SIGs) are a possibility, as are similar project plans, but expert judgment is considered the best answer because of the technical detail that can be provided by a subject matter expert.

9. Your current project has produced a requirements management plan. What is the purpose of this document?

   A. The requirements management plan links requirements to their origin and traces them throughout the project.

   B. The requirements management plan documents how requirements will be analyzed, documented, and managed throughout the project.

   C. The requirements management plan describes how individual requirements meet the business need for the project.

   D. The requirements management plan provides guidance on how project scope will be defined, documented, verified, managed, and controlled.

   ☑ **B.** The requirements management plan documents how requirements will be analyzed, documented, and managed throughout the project.

   ☒ **A**, **C**, and **D** are incorrect. **A** is incorrect because it is the definition of the requirements traceability matrix, not the requirements management plan. **C** is incorrect because it describes the requirements document. **D** is incorrect because it describes the scope management plan.

10. Which three Project Scope Management processes use the project charter as an input?

    A. Plan Scope Management, Create WBS, and Validate Scope

    B. Create WBS, Validate Scope, and Control Scope

    C. Control Scope, Define Scope, and Collect Requirements

    D. Plan Scope Management, Collect Requirements, and Define Scope

    ☑ **D.** The three processes that use the project charter as an input in the Project Scope Management process group are Plan Scope Management, Collect Requirements, and Define Scope.

    ☒ **A**, **B**, and **C** are incorrect because each contains the wrong combination of the exact three processes that use the project charter as an input in the Project Scope Management process group: Plan Scope Management, Collect Requirements, and Define Scope.

11. Which Project Scope Management process uses only data analysis as a tool and technique?

    A. Plan Scope Management

    B. Collect Requirements

    C. Define Scope

    D. Control Scope

    ☑ **D.** The Control Scope process within the Project Scope Management process group uses only data analysis as a technique to perform variance analysis and trend analysis.

    ☒ **A, B,** and **C** are incorrect because while each of these processes within the Project Scope Management process group uses data analysis techniques, they also use additional techniques; Control Scope is the only process to use only data analysis as a technique to perform variance analysis and trend analysis.

12. Which Project Scope Management process creates the scope baseline?

    A. Plan Scope Management

    B. Control Scope

    C. Create WBS

    D. Validate Scope

    ☑ **C.** The scope baseline is an output of the Create WBS process within the Project Scope Management process group.

    ☒ **A, B,** and **D** are incorrect because the scope baseline is created as an output of the Create WBS process within the Project Scope Management process group and is not an output of Plan Scope Management, Control Scope, or Validate Scope.

13. Your current project has multiple stakeholders representing each of the departments. In this case, who would approve the scope statement that you develop?

    A. The project team members

    B. The project sponsor

    C. The project manager

    D. The financial manager

    ☑ **B.** The project sponsors or initiators drive the business need for the project, and they approve the project scope statement.

    ☒ **A, C,** and **D** are incorrect. **A** is incorrect because while project team members may provide input to the project scope statement, they are not approvers. **C** is incorrect because the project manager has created the project scope statement and must seek approval from the project sponsor. **D** is incorrect because while the financial manager has input to creating the scope statement, approving their own input would be inappropriate.

14. What action should the project manager take when finding out the organization lacks a formal requirements management process that can accommodate the current project?

   A. Pause the project and create a formal requirements management process.

   B. Tailor the way the Project Scope Management processes are applied.

   C. Purchase a commercial off-the-shelf requirements management tool.

   D. Add requirements to the SharePoint repository as an alternative.

   ☑ **B.** The project manager has latitude to tailor the way the Project Scope Management processes are applied to accommodate both formal and informal requirements management processes.

   ☒ **A, C,** and **D** are incorrect. **A** is incorrect because pausing the current project to take on a different project (one to create a formal requirements management process) is not recommended, as there is no business need stated, nor is this the project manager's decision. **C** is incorrect because simply purchasing a software tool will be inadequate to the task of formalizing the requirements management project; it requires a cultural change. **D** is incorrect because the question does not indicate that SharePoint is an option, nor is SharePoint alone a solution to formalizing a requirements management process.

15. What is the project manager tailoring if he or she is deciding to use an adaptive, predictive, or hybrid approach?

   A. Validation and control approach

   B. Governance approach

   C. Procurement approach

   D. Development approach

   ☑ **D.** The development approach involves deciding among agile, predictive, and hybrid approaches.

   ☒ **A, B,** and **C** are incorrect. **A** is incorrect because the validation and control approach talks about how to do the specific parts of validating and controlling, while agile/predictive/hybrid address the entire project approach. **B** is incorrect because governance is about the decision making, change control, and escalation approaches. **C** is incorrect because procurement is a process that may take place, regardless of whether an agile/predictive/hybrid development approach is chosen.

16. Which of the following can help unstable requirements move to the point of being stable and well defined?

   A. Lean techniques

   B. RACI chart

   C. Project management plan

   D. Root-cause analysis

☑ **A** is correct because lean, agile, or other adaptive techniques are a tailoring approach for moving unstable requirements to stable, well-defined requirements.

☒ **B, C,** and **D** are incorrect. **B** is incorrect because a RACI chart is about roles and responsibilities of stakeholders. **C** is incorrect because the project management plan is not a technique focused on stabilizing requirements. **D** is incorrect because the question does not indicate an underlying problem that must be resolved.

17. When examining the validation and control mechanisms in place for the current project, what should a project manager be looking to tailor if appropriate for the project?

   A. Governance approaches

   B. Control-related policies, procedures, and guidelines

   C. Change control for requirements

   D. Matrix management

   ☑ **B.** This is a tailoring option to modify the validation and control processes by adapting control-related policies, procedures, and guidelines.

   ☒ **A, C,** and **D** are incorrect because none are directly related to the validation and control processes.

18. Which of the following is considered a primary purpose of a project's WBS?

   A. Clarify the responsibility for project tasks.

   B. Communicate with all stakeholders.

   C. Define the business need for the project.

   D. Detail the dates for the work packages.

   ☑ **B** is correct because the WBS serves as a communication mechanism to and from project stakeholders.

   ☒ **A, C,** and **D** are incorrect. **A** is incorrect because the WBS does not show responsibilities for tasks. **C** is incorrect because the business need is defined in the project charter. **D** is incorrect because dates are based on more detailed schedule planning.

19. Project management office support deliverables should be considered which of the following in the WBS?

   A. Top-level milestone

   B. External deliverable

   C. Work package

   D. Project management artifact

   ☑ **C.** The effort to create project management office support deliverables is indeed work and therefore should be represented in the WBS as a work package. A work package is a group of related tasks within a project. Work packages are the smallest unit of work (typically 8 to 80 hours) that a project can be broken down into when creating a work breakdown structure (WBS).

☒ **A**, **B**, and **D** are incorrect. **A** is incorrect because a high-level milestone is a deliverable or major event to be achieved on a specified date. **B** is incorrect because an external deliverable is a product, service, or result delivered to a customer outside the company. **D** is incorrect because project management artifacts are created when carrying out the work packages in a WBS (e.g., user stories, class diagrams, Unified Modeling Language models).

20. Your project requires that you hire multiple third-party vendors, and you are considering elements to include in the procurement management plan for the project. Before completing the procurement management plan, you should first:

    A. Review project assets on procurement

    B. Develop activity cost estimates

    C. Prepare a prequalified seller list

    D. Review the WBS

    ☑ **D.** The procurement management plan is a part of the overall project management plan, and the WBS is the best predictor of the success of a new project, including vendor assets. By reviewing the work breakdown structure before you prepare the procurement plan, it is relatively easy to determine what procurements are needed throughout the life of the project. The WBS identifies items to be procured, and the procurement plan defines the items to be procured, the types of contracts to be used in support of the project, the contract approval process, and decision criteria.

    ☒ **A**, **B**, and **C** are incorrect. **A** is incorrect because you are not at the point that assets for procurement would be available. **B** is incorrect because you prepare activity cost estimates after you create the WBS. **C** is incorrect because a prequalified seller list is prepared in conducting procurements, which follows the creation of the procurement management plan.

21. What does the 100 percent rule refer to?

    A. The ratio of requirements that need to be implemented for the project to be a success

    B. The sum of quality tasks in a project together with the administrative tasks

    C. The presence of all product and project work in the WBS with nothing left out and no extra work included

    D. The ratio of stakeholder engagement required for the project to move to the Executing phase

    ☑ **C.** The 100 percent rule refers to the premise that the WBS represents all product and project work with nothing left out and no extra work included.

    ☒ **A**, **B**, and **D** are incorrect. **A** is incorrect because there is no steadfast percentage or ratio of requirements that lead to project success; instead, stakeholder satisfaction is the guide. **B** is incorrect because the focus on just quality tasks and administrative tasks misses all the product development tasks. **D** is incorrect because moving to the Executing phase of a process is not dependent solely on the engagement of stakeholders; many other items are important, such as completing the project management plan.

22. Which of the following is a generally accepted business practice used in creating a project's WBS?

A. Structure it so product scope and project scope are easily managed.

B. Set it up to show the complete scope of the work to be carried out on the project.

C. Use it to define the management control points for each of the major deliverables.

D. Define the solution to the problem in terms of a product, service, or result.

☑ B. The WBS is the total and complete scope of work to be done on the project—in other words, what is *in* scope.

☒ A, C, and D are incorrect. A is incorrect because product scope is the features and functions of the product. The WBS is the work performed to deliver the product and provides the framework of what must be delivered. C is incorrect because management control points are normally key review points, such as end of design, or a major management review, such as a review performed after the release of the risk management plan. D is incorrect because the "how," or solution to the problem, is left to the technical team after the business team has described the "what," or purpose of the product, service, or result.

23. Your team has chosen a user story to prototype for an area of high risk in the project. Which of the following *best* describes the process in which you are involved?

A. Calculating the total duration of the project from the start

B. Counting the total number of work packages in the project

C. Allocating responsibilities for the project work to individuals in the team

D. Subdividing the project work into smaller, more manageable components

☑ D. The Create WBS process subdivides the major project deliverables and project work into smaller, more manageable components.

☒ A, B, and C are incorrect. A is incorrect because the WBS does not concern project duration. B is incorrect because determining the total work package count is not a function of the Create WBS process. C is incorrect because the allocation of responsibilities is not a function of the initial WBS.

24. In an agile project, who decides who will perform the work for the next period's defined scope?

A. Product owner

B. Project manager

C. Scrum Master

D. Team members

☑ **D.** In self-organizing teams prevalent in the agile/adaptive approach to projects, team members decide who will do the work required for the iteration/period/sprint to complete the identified scope for that period.

☒ **A, B,** and **C** are incorrect. **A** and **B** are incorrect because the product owner and sometimes the project manager identify and prioritize the scope for an iteration/period/sprint but will not decide who performs what work within the project team. **C** is incorrect because the role of Scrum Master is specific to the agile Scrum methodology and is only in charge of ensuring the sprint follows Scrum guidelines properly.

25. Which of the following allows agile teams to see what they've accomplished and shows changes in scope during an iteration?

A. Product backlog

B. Burnup chart

C. RACI chart

D. Control chart

☑ **B.** The burnup chart shows changes in scope during an iteration and allows teams to see what they have accomplished, helping the team proceed to the next piece of work.

☒ **A, C,** and **D** are incorrect. **A** is incorrect because a product backlog shows the entire set of work still to be done for the project. **C** is incorrect because a RACI chart is specific to the roles and responsibilities of project stakeholders. **D** is incorrect because a control chart is used as a data representation to perform the Control Quality process.

26. In developing project scope, one approach is to:

A. Describe scope in user stories

B. Determine scope through high-level infrastructure

C. Use the project's budget to set a financial baseline

D. Include nonfunctional requirements for products, services, or results

☑ **A.** In the adaptive approach, you are more likely to create a scope statement as project requirements in terms of user stories, as compared to a functional requirements document created as part of a predictive lifecycle project.

☒ **B, C,** and **D** are incorrect. **B** is incorrect because the high-level infrastructure is determined as part of high-level design (HLD). Scope will drive the design. **C** is incorrect because the project's budget is used to set a cost performance baseline. **D** is incorrect because nonfunctional requirements (speed, maintainability, robustness, etc.) are classified as solution requirements and are documented when collecting requirements.

27. You have made the decision to control risk through planning on your current project and therefore conclude that your scope management approach should be:

A. Predictive

B. Adaptive

C. Iterative

D. Lean

☑ **A.** In a predictive (plan-driven) lifecycle, the three major constraints (scope, schedule, and cost) are determined ahead of time, and not just at a high level, but in detail. This is where the high-level planning is done for the entire project, but the detailed planning is done only for the work that needs to be done soon. In a plan-driven lifecycle, the detailed scope of the project is determined right from the start.

☒ **B, C,** and **D** are incorrect. **B** and **C** are incorrect because the adaptive lifecycle is based upon the iterative and incremental process models and focuses upon adaptability to changing product requirements and enhancing customer satisfaction through rapid delivery of working product features and client participation. **D** is incorrect because lean is also an adaptive lifecycle approach and controls risk through rapid delivery of small amounts of working product.

CHAPTER 6

Project Schedule Management

In this chapter, you will

- Define the six project management processes in the Project Schedule Management knowledge area
- Identify the input, tools, techniques, and outputs defined in the six processes in Project Schedule Management
- Solve simple network diagrams problems and perform basic scheduling calculations
- Identify considerations for agile/adaptive environments in Project Schedule Management

The Project Schedule Management knowledge area accounts for 9 percent (27) of the questions on the CAPM exam. The *PMBOK Guide, Sixth Edition,* Sections 6.1 through 6.6, cover the six processes in the Project Schedule Management knowledge area.

This chapter focuses on the topic of project schedule (time) management. Project Schedule Management, like the other knowledge areas, begins with a process of planning that produces a schedule management plan. Then there is an iterative, or repeating, process that produces and updates the project schedule. Then, as with all other knowledge areas except for the Project Resource Management knowledge area, there is a controlling process that seeks to measure planned versus actual progress in relation to the schedule (time) and deal with any changes or corrective or preventive actions.

You may need to pay attention in this chapter to those activities that lead up to the construction of the network diagram, because there is quite a bit of technical information that you will need to learn.

Project Schedule Management is focused upon the processes of developing a schedule management plan, preparing your project schedule, ensuring that the project progresses as planned and that milestones are reached on the communicated schedule, and influencing and assessing any changes to the project schedule.

Apart from the Control Schedule process, the processes contained in this knowledge area present what appears to be a wonderfully logical and sequential flow of information, from defining the activities through to development of the project schedule. Estimating durations for activities and the overall project is done in the Project Resource Management knowledge area.

The 27 practice questions in this chapter are mapped to the style and frequency of question types you will see on the CAPM exam.

1. What is the correct order of processes in the Project Schedule Management knowledge area?

    A. Define Activities, Sequence Activities, Estimate Activity Durations, Develop Schedule

    B. Define Activities, Estimate Activity Durations, Sequence Activities, Develop Schedule

    C. Sequence Activities, Define Activities, Estimate Activity Durations, Develop Schedule

    D. Define Activities, Sequence Activities, Develop Schedule, Estimate Activity Durations

2. What is the document that provides additional information about activities identified on the activity list?

    A. Project charter

    B. Activities attributes

    C. Resource breakdown structure

    D. Scope statement

3. What is the best definition of rolling wave planning?

    A. It is the breakdown of work packages into activities.

    B. It is a form of progressive elaboration that focuses on defining work in the immediate future in more detail than work further off.

    C. It is the process of first defining, then sequencing, then estimating durations in the preparation of the project schedule.

    D. It is the process of comparing actual progress against planned progress.

4. What is the name of the document that will guide the definition, documentation, execution, and control of the project schedule?

    A. Project management plan

    B. Scope statement

    C. Organizational process assets

    D. Schedule management plan

5. Why are activity resources generally estimated before activity durations?

    A. Because that is the way the *PMBOK Guide* sets them out.

    B. Because to estimate activity durations, you must know what sequence they occur in.

    C. Because you need to know how many resources are available to complete an activity, because this will affect how fast the activity can be completed.

    D. They do not; it is better to estimate activity durations first, then estimate activity resources.

6. What is the form of estimating that uses known quantities and multiplies them by known metrics?

A. Analogous estimating

B. Parametric estimating

C. Three-point estimating

D. The Delphi technique

7. What sort of estimating technique are you using when you are obtaining information from a group of experts about your project durations, and each expert is being asked individually for their opinion without knowing who else is being interviewed?

A. Alternatives analysis

B. Parametric estimating

C. Three-point estimating

D. The Delphi technique

8. Which of the following estimating techniques is part of the PERT technique?

A. Analogous estimating

B. Parametric estimating

C. Three-point estimating

D. Bottom-up estimating

9. If a successor activity cannot start until its predecessor activity has started, what sort of relationship is this?

A. Finish-to-start

B. Start-to-start

C. Finish-to-finish

D. Start-to-finish

10. What is the name of the process of considering whether an additional amount of time should be provided based on quantitative risk analysis?

A. Expert judgment

B. Parametric estimating

C. Reserve analysis

D. Monte Carlo analysis

11. The path, or paths, through a project schedule network that represent the most risk because there is no total float is called what?

A. Critical chain

B. Network diagram

C. Gantt chart

D. Critical path

12. If you are compressing the project schedule by using a technique that generally does not increase project costs, which of the following techniques are you using?

   A. Fast tracking

   B. Crashing

   C. Resource optimization

   D. Resource leveling

13. The amount of time a successor activity must wait after the completion of its predecessor activity is known as what?

   A. Lead

   B. Resource leveling

   C. Lag

   D. Float

14. Which of the following is not contained in the activity list?

   A. Milestone list

   B. Scope of work description

   C. All schedule activities required on the project

   D. Activity identifier

15. Which of the following is the most commonly used type of precedence relationship that you will use?

   A. Start-to-start

   B. Start-to-finish

   C. Finish-to-finish

   D. Finish-to-start

16. You have scheduled two activities in your project so that the successor activity is able to start a week before the predecessor activity. What is this an example of?

   A. Lag

   B. Lead

   C. Slack

   D. Float

17. You are completing the sequence of activities and note that one of your activities cannot proceed until consent is granted by the local government agency. This is an example of what sort of dependency?

   A. Discretionary

   B. External

C. Environmental

D. Mandatory

18. What sort of information is included in your resource calendar?

    A. The length of time the project will require input from external resources

    B. The dates of annual holidays for project team members

    C. The duration of each activity in the project resource diagram

    D. When and how long project resources will be available during the project

19. As a result of a brainstorming session, your team determines that the most likely duration of an activity will be 8 days, the optimistic duration is 6 days, and the pessimistic duration is 16 days. What is the expected activity duration?

    A. 10 days

    B. 5 days

    C. 9 days

    D. 30 days

20. To estimate the amount of time it will take to install 500 meters of cable on your project, you divide the number of meters required by how many meters an hour the person laying the cable can lay. This is an example of which sort of tool or technique?

    A. Three-point estimating

    B. Bottom-up estimating

    C. Analogous estimating

    D. Parametric estimating

21. What is the *PMBOK Guide* process of analyzing activity sequences, durations, resource requirements, and scheduled constraints to create the project schedule?

    A. Project Schedule Development

    B. Create Project Schedule

    C. Develop Schedule

    D. Schedule Management

22. Of the following which best describes a Gantt chart?

    A. The best tool to view activity sequencing

    B. A chart that shows activities and their levels of effort

    C. A chart that represents daily activities

    D. A tool to view the sequence of low-level activities

23. You are using a methodology that calculates the amount of float on various paths in the network diagram to determine the minimum project duration. What tool or technique are you using?

    A. Critical path method

    B. Critical chain method

    C. Parametric estimating

    D. Three-point estimating

24. You are using a computer-based modeling technique that examines the possible outcomes based on a range of potential probabilities if a particular situation occurs. What is this technique called?

    A. Parametric estimating

    B. Schedule compression

    C. Critical chain method

    D. What-if scenario analysis

25. What is the name of the process in the *PMBOK Guide* that monitors the status of the project to update project progress and manage changes to the schedule baseline?

    A. Develop Schedule

    B. Monitoring and Controlling

    C. Verify Schedule

    D. Control Schedule

26. What does a schedule performance index (SPI) of 0.9 mean?

    A. The amount of buffer in your critical chain methodology is less than optimal.

    B. The project network diagram was incorrectly put together.

    C. The project is behind schedule and in need of schedule compression.

    D. The project is ahead of schedule.

27. Yvette has requested that each team member determine the estimates by multiplying the quantity of work to be performed by the known historical productivity rate of the individual department. What is this technique called?

    A. Parametric estimating

    B. Analogous estimating

    C. Three-point estimating

    D. Expert judgment

1. A	**10.** C	**19.** C
2. B	**11.** D	**20.** D
3. B	**12.** A	**21.** C
4. D	**13.** C	**22.** D
5. C	**14.** A	**23.** A
6. B	**15.** D	**24.** D
7. D	**16.** B	**25.** D
8. C	**17.** B	**26.** C
9. B	**18.** D	**27.** A

1. What is the correct order of processes in the Project Schedule Management knowledge area?

   A. Define Activities, Sequence Activities, Estimate Activity Durations, Develop Schedule

   B. Define Activities, Estimate Activity Durations, Sequence Activities, Develop Schedule

   C. Sequence Activities, Define Activities, Estimate Activity Durations, Develop Schedule

   D. Define Activities, Sequence Activities, Develop Schedule, Estimate Activity Durations

   ☑ **A**. First define activities, then estimate durations, then sequence them, then develop the schedule.

   ☒ **B, C**, and **D** are incorrect. **B** is incorrect because Estimate Activity Durations generally occurs after Sequence Activities in the Project Resource Management knowledge area. **C** is incorrect because Sequence Activities occurs after Define Activities. **D** is incorrect because Develop Schedule occurs after Estimate Activity Durations.

2. What is the document that provides additional information about activities identified on the activity list?

   A. Project charter

   B. Activities attributes

   C. Resource breakdown structure

   D. Scope statement

   ☑ **B**. The activities attributes document provides additional detail about identified activities.

   ☒ **A, C**, and **D** are incorrect. **A** is incorrect because the project charter contains high-level information. **C** is incorrect because the resource breakdown structure provides a breakdown of categories and types of resources required on the project. **D** is incorrect because the scope statement describes all the work to be done on the project.

3. What is the best definition of rolling wave planning?

   A. It is the breakdown of work packages into activities.

   B. It is a form of progressive elaboration that focuses on defining work in the immediate future in more detail than work further off.

   C. It is the process of first defining, then sequencing, then estimating durations in the preparation of the project schedule.

   D. It is the process of comparing actual progress against planned progress.

   ☑ **B**. It is a form of progressive elaboration that focuses on defining work in the immediate future in more detail than work further off.

   ☒ **A, C**, and **D** are incorrect. **A** is incorrect because the breakdown of work packages into activities is the process of Decomposition. **C** is incorrect because the process of first defining, then sequencing, then estimating durations in the preparation of the project schedule broadly outlines the Time Management processes. **D** is incorrect because the process of comparing actual progress against planned progress is Variance Analysis.

4. What is the name of the document that will guide the definition, documentation, execution, and control of the project schedule?

    A. Project management plan

    B. Scope statement

    C. Organizational process assets

    D. Schedule management plan

    ☑ **D.** The schedule management plan defines how the project schedule will be developed, executed, and controlled.

    ☒ **A, B,** and **C** are incorrect. **A** is incorrect because the project management plan is the plan containing many subsidiary plans and documents. **B** is incorrect because the scope statement defines the work to be done on the project. **C** is incorrect because the organizational process assets are process polices, templates, and methodologies the wider organization owns and are used to assist project management.

5. Why are activity resources generally estimated before activity durations?

    A. Because that is the way the *PMBOK Guide* sets them out.

    B. Because to estimate activity durations, you must know what sequence they occur in.

    C. Because you need to know how many resources are available to complete an activity, because this will affect how fast the activity can be completed.

    D. They do not; it is better to estimate activity durations first, then estimate activity resources.

    ☑ **C.** You need to know how many resources are available to complete an activity because this will affect how fast the activity can be completed.

    ☒ **A, B,** and **D** are incorrect. **A** is incorrect because the *PMBOK Guide* is not prescriptive. **B** is incorrect because this answer links two processes that are separated by the Estimate Activity Resources process (which is in the Project Resource Management knowledge area). **D** is incorrect because generally, it's better to estimate activity resources (which is in the Project Resource Management knowledge area) first and then estimate activity durations.

6. What is the form of estimating that uses known quantities and multiplies them by known metrics?

    A. Analogous estimating

    B. Parametric estimating

    C. Three-point estimating

    D. The Delphi technique

    ☑ **B.** Parametric estimating uses known quantities and multiplies them by known metrics.

☒ **A**, **C**, and **D** are incorrect. **A** is incorrect because analogous estimating uses a similar activity to estimate the resources or duration of a current activity. **C** is incorrect because three-point estimating uses a weighted average of an optimistic, most likely, and pessimistic estimate. **D** is incorrect because the Delphi technique solicits information from experts anonymously.

7. What sort of estimating technique are you using when you are obtaining information from a group of experts about your project durations, and each expert is being asked individually for their opinion without knowing who else is being interviewed?

   A. Alternatives analysis

   B. Parametric estimating

   C. Three-point estimating

   D. The Delphi technique

   ☑ **D.** The Delphi technique solicits information from experts anonymously.

   ☒ **A**, **B**, and **C** are incorrect. **A** is incorrect because alternatives analysis considers a range of alternative approaches to determine the most appropriate one. **B** is incorrect because parametric estimating uses known quantities and multiplies them by known metrics. **C** is incorrect because three-point estimating uses a weighted average of an optimistic, most likely, and pessimistic estimate.

8. Which of the following estimating techniques is part of the PERT technique?

   A. Analogous estimating

   B. Parametric estimating

   C. Three-point estimating

   D. Bottom-up estimating

   ☑ **C.** Three-point estimating uses a weighted average of an optimistic, most likely, and pessimistic estimate and is part of the program evaluation and review technique (PERT).

   ☒ **A**, **B**, and **D** are incorrect. **A** is incorrect because analogous estimating uses a similar activity to estimate the resources or duration of a current activity. **B** is incorrect because parametric estimating uses known quantities and multiplies them by known metrics. **D** is incorrect because bottom-up estimating aggregates low-level estimates and rolls them up to obtain higher-level estimates.

9. If a successor activity cannot start until its predecessor activity has started, what sort of relationship is this?

   A. Finish-to-start

   B. Start-to-start

   C. Finish-to-finish

   D. Start-to-finish

☑ **B**. A start-to-start relationship means a successor activity cannot start until its predecessor activity has started.

☒ **A, C,** and **D** are incorrect. **A** is incorrect because a finish-to-start relationship means the successor cannot start until the predecessor finishes. **C** is incorrect because a finish-to-finish relationship means the successor cannot finish until the predecessor finishes. **D** is incorrect because a start-to-finish relationship means the successor cannot finish until the predecessor starts.

10. What is the name of the process of considering whether an additional amount of time should be provided based on quantitative risk analysis?

   A. Expert judgment

   B. Parametric estimating

   C. Reserve analysis

   D. Monte Carlo analysis

   ☑ **C**. Reserve analysis considers whether an additional amount of time should be provided based on quantitative risk analysis.

   ☒ **A, B,** and **D** are incorrect. **A** is incorrect because expert judgment is a technique for getting information from acknowledged experts. **B** is incorrect because parametric estimating uses known quantities and multiplies them by known metrics. **D** is incorrect because Monte Carlo analysis uses sophisticated mathematical modeling to forecast future states from observed data.

11. The path, or paths, through a project schedule network that represent the most risk because there is no total float is called what?

   A. Critical chain

   B. Network diagram

   C. Gantt chart

   D. Critical path

   ☑ **D**. The critical path is the path, or paths, through a project schedule network that represent the most risk because there is no total float.

   ☒ **A, B,** and **C** are incorrect. **A** is incorrect because the critical chain method places time buffers around high-risk activities to mitigate any potential adverse impact on the project duration. **B** is incorrect because the network diagram is a graphical representation of the project activities and the relationship between them. **C** is incorrect because the Gantt chart is a graphical representation of the project schedule.

12. If you are compressing the project schedule by using a technique that generally does not increase project costs, which of the following techniques are you using?
    A. Fast tracking
    B. Crashing
    C. Resource optimization
    D. Resource leveling

    ☑ **A.** Fast tracking schedules activities in parallel that would normally be done in sequence.

    ☒ **B, C,** and **D** are incorrect. **B** is incorrect because crashing adds more resources to an activity to shorten its duration, but it usually costs money. **C** is incorrect because resource optimization is a technique of making most efficient use of resources on a project. **D** is incorrect because resource leveling is a type of resource optimization.

13. The amount of time a successor activity must wait after the completion of its predecessor activity is known as what?
    A. Lead
    B. Resource leveling
    C. Lag
    D. Float

    ☑ **C.** The lag is the amount of time a successor activity must wait after the completion of its predecessor activity.

    ☒ **A, B,** and **D** are incorrect. **A** is incorrect because lead is the amount of time a successor can start before completion of the predecessor activity. **B** is incorrect because resource leveling is a type of resource optimization. **D** is incorrect because the float is the amount of time an activity can be delayed before it has an impact upon successor activities or the total project duration.

14. Which of the following is not contained in the activity list?
    A. Milestone list
    B. Scope of work description
    C. All schedule activities required on the project
    D. Activity identifier

    ☑ **A.** The milestone list would be found in your WBS dictionary.

    ☒ **B, C,** and **D** are incorrect. **B** is incorrect because the scope of work description is contained in the activity list. **C** is incorrect because all schedule activities required on the project are contained in the activity list. **D** is incorrect because activity identifiers are contained in the activity list.

15. Which of the following is the most commonly used type of precedence relationship that you will use?

A. Start-to-start

B. Start-to-finish

C. Finish-to-finish

D. Finish-to-start

☑ **D.** Finish-to-start means that the successor activity can't start until its predecessor activity is finished. Most activities have this sort of relationship.

☒ **A**, **B**, and **C** are incorrect. **A** is incorrect because start-to-start is not the most common type of relationship. **B** is incorrect because very few activities have start-to-finish relationships, which means that the successor activity cannot finish until its predecessor activity starts. **C** is incorrect because finish-to-finish is not the most common type of relationship.

16. You have scheduled two activities in your project so that the successor activity is able to start a week before the predecessor activity. What is this an example of?

A. Lag

B. Lead

C. Slack

D. Float

☑ **B.** A lead means that one activity can get started before its predecessor finishes even though it has a finish-to-start relationship. It would be shown on a network diagram as having a finish-to-start relationship with a week lead time.

☒ **A**, **C**, and **D** are incorrect. **A** is incorrect because lag refers to the amount of time a successor activity must wait after the end of its predecessor before it can start. **C** is incorrect because slack refers to the amount of time that an activity can be delayed before it affects successor activities' start dates. It is one of the few instances in the *PMBOK Guide* where two terms, slack and float, are interchangeable. **D** is incorrect because float refers to the amount of time that an activity can be delayed before it affects successor activities' start dates. It is one of the few instances in the *PMBOK Guide* where two terms, slack and float, are interchangeable.

17. You are completing the sequence of activities and note that one of your activities cannot proceed until consent is granted by the local government agency. This is an example of what sort of dependency?

A. Discretionary

B. External

C. Environmental

D. Mandatory

☑ **B.** An external dependency means that you are waiting on work being done by people or organizations outside of the project.

☒ **A**, **C**, and **D** are incorrect. **A** is incorrect because a discretionary dependency is one where a successor should come after the predecessor but there is some discretion, particularly if a schedule requires compression to shorten duration. **C** is incorrect because there is no such term as environmental dependency in the *PMBOK Guide*. **D** is incorrect because mandatory dependency means that the successor must come after the predecessor. A mandatory dependency is also one that is internal, not external, to the project.

18. What sort of information is included in your resource calendar?

    A. The length of time the project will require input from external resources

    B. The dates of annual holidays for project team members

    C. The duration of each activity in the project resource diagram

    D. When and how long project resources will be available during the project

    ☑ **D.** Your resource calendar is a useful input into the Estimate Activity Resources process, and it clearly shows when and where resources will be available to the project.

    ☒ **A**, **B**, and **C** are incorrect. **A** is incorrect because the length of time the project will require input from external resources is not shown in the resource calendar. This would be part of the information shown in the network schedule. **B** is incorrect because the dates of annual holidays for project team members would be a part of the information included in the resource calendar, but it is not the best answer available. **C** is incorrect because the resource calendar does not show the duration of each activity. This would be shown in the network schedule.

19. As a result of a brainstorming session, your team determines that the most likely duration of an activity will be 8 days, the optimistic duration is 6 days, and the pessimistic duration is 16 days. What is the expected activity duration?

    A. 10 days

    B. 5 days

    C. 9 days

    D. 30 days

    ☑ **C.** Using three-point estimating, the expected duration is: $(6 + (8 \times 4) + 16)/6 = 9$ days.

    ☒ **A**, **B**, and **D** are incorrect because, using three-point estimating, the expected duration is: $(6 + (8 \times 4) + 16)/6 = 9$ days.

20. To estimate the amount of time it will take to install 500 meters of cable on your project, you divide the number of meters required by how many meters an hour the person laying the cable can lay. This is an example of which sort of tool or technique?

    A. Three-point estimating

    B. Bottom-up estimating

C. Analogous estimating

D. Parametric estimating

☑ **D.** Parametric estimating uses numbers and quantifiable measures to estimate. Remember, if you see the word *metric*, it means number or measure.

☒ **A**, **B**, and **C** are incorrect. **A** is incorrect because this is not an example of three-point estimating. Three-point estimating uses the optimistic, realistic, and pessimistic estimates to calculate a weight average. **B** is incorrect because this is not an example of bottom-up estimating. Bottom-up estimating breaks down work packages and activities into the smallest possible piece of work and then adds up the time and cost for each to get a total project cost or duration. **C** is incorrect because this is not an example of analogous estimating. Analogous estimating involves using information from similar projects (i.e., an analogy) to estimate elements of your project and is generally less costly and time consuming than other techniques.

21. What is the *PMBOK Guide* process of analyzing activity sequences, durations, resource requirements, and scheduled constraints to create the project schedule?

A. Project Schedule Development

B. Create Project Schedule

C. Develop Schedule

D. Schedule Management

☑ **C.** This is the final stage in the Planning process group for the Project Time Management knowledge area. It takes all the previous information from the previous planning processes and makes the project schedule. This process will be quite iterative because at the start of the project the information you have available is less accurate.

☒ **A**, **B**, and **D** are incorrect because they are not the name of *PMBOK Guide* processes.

22. Of the following which best describes a Gantt chart?

A. The best tool to view activity sequencing

B. A chart that shows activities and their levels of effort

C. A chart that represents daily activities

D. A tool to view the sequence of low-level activities

☑ **D.** A Gantt chart is a chart used to track day-to-day activities. It can also be called a bar chart.

☒ **A**, **B**, and **C** are incorrect. **A** is incorrect because the best tool to view activity sequencing is a network precedence diagram. **B** is incorrect because a Gantt chart shows activities on the vertical axis, dates on the horizontal axis, and activity durations are shown on horizontal bars placed according to start and finish dates. **C** is incorrect because a Gantt chart represents activities, durations, and dates.

23. You are using a methodology that calculates the amount of float on various paths in the network diagram to determine the minimum project duration. What tool or technique are you using?

A. Critical path method

B. Critical chain method

C. Parametric estimating

D. Three-point estimating

☑ **A.** Critical path methodology focuses on the amount of float in network paths to determine the critical path through a project. The critical path has no float associated with it and as such represents the greatest risk to the project duration.

☒ **B, C,** and **D** are incorrect. **B** is incorrect because the critical chain method is a schedule network analysis technique that modifies a project schedule to account for limited resources by deliberately adding in nonworking time buffers, which is intended to protect the target finish date from slippage along the critical chain. **C** is incorrect because parametric estimating is a process that multiplies known quantities by known financial rates. **D** is incorrect because three-point estimating uses the pessimistic, realistic, and optimistic estimates to get a weight average.

24. You are using a computer-based modeling technique that examines the possible outcomes based on a range of potential probabilities if a particular situation occurs. What is this technique called?

A. Parametric estimating

B. Schedule compression

C. Critical chain method

D. What-if scenario analysis

☑ **D.** A what-if scenario analysis runs through all the different outcomes if a particular scenario occurs. This level of information can assist with many types of estimating to get the full range of possibilities. The most comprehensive type of what-if scenario analysis is a Monte Carlo analysis.

☒ **A, B,** and **C** are incorrect. **A** is incorrect because this is not an example of parametric estimating. Parametric estimating is a process that multiplies known quantities by known financial rates. **B** is incorrect because schedule compression involves using fast tracking or crashing to reduce the project duration. **C** is incorrect because the critical chain method is a schedule network analysis technique that modifies a project schedule to account for limited resources by deliberately adding in nonworking time buffers, which is intended to protect the target finish date from slippage along the critical chain.

25. What is the name of the process in the *PMBOK Guide* that monitors the status of the project to update project progress and manage changes to the schedule baseline?

A. Develop Schedule

B. Monitoring and Controlling

C. Verify Schedule

D. Control Schedule

☑ **D.** Control Schedule is the only time management knowledge area process that appears in the Monitoring and Controlling process group.

☒ **A**, **B**, and **C** are incorrect. **A** is incorrect because the Develop Schedule process produces the project schedule and schedule baseline. **B** is incorrect because Monitoring and Controlling is a process group, not an individual process. **C** is incorrect because it is a made-up process name.

26. What does a schedule performance index (SPI) of 0.9 mean?

A. The amount of buffer in your critical chain methodology is less than optimal.

B. The project network diagram was incorrectly put together.

C. The project is behind schedule and in need of schedule compression.

D. The project is ahead of schedule.

☑ **C.** An SPI of 1 means the project is on schedule, less than 1 means behind schedule, and greater than 1 means ahead of schedule.

☒ **A**, **B**, and **D** are incorrect. **A** is incorrect because this calculation does not immediately tell you if your amount of buffer is less than optimal. **B** is incorrect because this calculation does not immediately tell you if your network diagram was incorrectly put together. **D** is incorrect because an SPI of 1 means the project is on schedule, less than 1 means behind schedule, and greater than 1 means ahead of schedule.

27. Yvette has requested that each team member determine the estimates by multiplying the quantity of work to be performed by the known historical productivity rate of the individual department. What is this technique called?

A. Parametric estimating

B. Analogous estimating

C. Three-point estimating

D. Expert judgment

☑ **A.** Parametric estimating is an estimating technique that uses a statistical relationship between historical data and other variables to calculate an estimate for activity parameters.

☒ **B**, **C**, and **D** are incorrect. **B** is incorrect because analogous estimating uses an analogy from a previous project and extrapolates from that an estimate for a current project. The question presents an example of parametric estimating. **C** is incorrect because three-point estimating uses the pessimistic, realistic, and optimistic estimates to get a weighted average. **D** is incorrect because expert judgment uses the experience of experts to assist in preparing estimates.

Project Cost Management

In this chapter, you will

- Understand the four project management processes in the Project Cost Management knowledge area
- Identify the inputs, tools, techniques, and outputs defined in the four processes in Project Cost Management
- Identify key concepts in Project Cost Management, including tailoring and special considerations for agile/adaptive environments
- Understand and apply basic forecasting and earned value methods for Project Cost Management

In the Project Cost Management processes, the project manager plans costs and schedules for the project. Early in a project, the initial budget and completion date are estimated. Creating good estimates cannot take place without good information from both the project team members and the key stakeholders. Information from project team members and key stakeholders provides the basis for estimates prepared by the project manager in order to fund and manage the resource costs and activities schedule.

The 27 practice questions in this chapter are mapped to the style and frequency of question types you will see on the CAPM exam.

1. Which of the following are often closely linked, particularly on smaller projects?
    A. Collecting requirements and testing product
    B. Planning the project and closing the project
    C. Cost estimating and cost budgeting
    D. Developing the team and managing the team

2. In which process does the project manager aggregate the estimated costs of individual activities in order to establish a cost baseline?
    A. Plan Cost Management
    B. Estimate Costs
    C. Determine Budget
    D. Control Costs

3. What is the key benefit of the Plan Cost Management process?
    A. Provides estimates for project costs at the beginning of the project
    B. Provides summary information to review project costs at the end of the project
    C. Provides ratios and variance analysis results reviewed at the end of the project
    D. Provides guidance on how project costs will be managed throughout the project

4. Which process creates an approximate monetary value for each project activity necessary to complete the work of the project?
    A. Plan Cost Management
    B. Estimate Costs
    C. Determine Budget
    D. Control Costs

5. What process are you performing if you are adding together the costs of individual activities into work packages and then rolling the work packages into control accounts and finishing with summarizing the control accounts?
    A. Plan Cost Management
    B. Estimate Costs
    C. Determine Budget
    D. Control Costs

6. In which process does the project manager perform a reserve analysis to account for unknown-unknown risks?
    A. Plan Cost Management
    B. Estimate Costs

    C. Determine Budget

    D. Control Costs

7. In which process is the project manager performing a variance analysis in order to take any necessary corrective actions to realign the project work with the project budget?

    A. Plan Cost Management

    B. Estimate Costs

    C. Determine Budget

    D. Control Costs

8. During project planning, you notice you do not have much information about one activity. You decide to estimate activity duration by referring to the actual duration of a similar activity on another project. This calculation method is called:

    A. Analogous estimating

    B. Expert judgment

    C. Parametric estimating

    D. Reserve analysis

9. Which technique are you using if you are calculating the theoretical early start and finish dates on your project schedule, along with late start and finish dates, for all the project activities?

    A. Critical chain method

    B. Critical path method

    C. Schedule compression

    D. What-if analysis

10. Your project sponsor for the current project expects to receive a narrow estimate for project costs because all project information is now known. Which of the following is considered a suitable range for this request?

    A. −100% to +100%

    B. −10% to +10%

    C. −25% to +25%

    D. −50% to +50%

11. You are calculating costs for your project based on costs from a previous similar project that was completed last month in your organization. This process is known as:

    A. Analogous estimating

    B. Bottom-up estimating

    C. Parametric estimating

    D. Three-point estimating

12. What estimation technique is your builder using if the cost has been presented to you as $100 per square foot?

   A. Analogous estimating

   B. Bottom-up estimating

   C. Parametric estimating

   D. Three-point estimating

13. Which estimation technique can make use of either triangular distribution or beta distribution?

   A. Analogous estimating

   B. Bottom-up estimating

   C. Parametric estimating

   D. Three-point estimating

14. Given a most likely value of 12, an optimistic value of 10, and a pessimistic value of 20, using the triangular distribution formula, what is the estimate for the task?

   A. 7

   B. 13

   C. 14

   D. 26

15. Which process group are you carrying out if you are primarily concerned with ensuring the project has the funds necessary for the resources needed to complete the project work?

   A. Project Scope Management

   B. Project Cost Management

   C. Project Resource Management

   D. Project Stakeholder Management

16. Which concern is being highlighted if the cost of an acquired item is allowed to be measured when the acquisition decision is made versus when the order is placed, versus when the item is delivered, versus when the actual cost is incurred?

   A. Different stakeholders measure project costs in different ways and at different times.

   B. Costs for a project cannot be accurately predicted.

   C. Project costs should have multiple values associated with each line item.

   D. Use multiple methods to measure costs and then aggregate all measurements.

17. What is the trend in Project Cost Management called Earned Schedules (ES) theory?

   A. Replaces the cost variance measure of Earned Value (EV) minus Planned Value (PV) with Earned Schedules (ES) minus Actual Time (AT)

   B. Replaces the cost variance measure of Earned Value (EV) plus Planned Value (PV) with Earned Schedules (ES) plus Actual Time (AT)

C. Replaces the schedule variance measure of Earned Value (EV) minus Planned Value (PV) with Earned Schedules (ES) minus Actual Time (AT)

D. Replaces the schedule variance measure of Earned Value (EV) plus Planned Value (PV) with Earned Schedules (ES) plus Actual Time (AT)

18. If your organization does not have an existing formal or informal cost estimation approach in place, what should you do as the project manager as a part of Project Cost Management?

A. Set a zero budget at the start of Project Cost Management and add costs to the budget as the project is progressively elaborated.

B. Transfer the responsibility for Project Cost Management to the PMO.

C. Set a budget that equals that of the previous project and update throughout the project.

D. Tailor the way Project Cost Management processes are applied.

19. When should a project manager make use of lightweight estimation methods to generate a high-level forecast of project labor costs?

A. On large projects

B. On small projects

C. On projects where the scope is fully defined

D. On projects with high degrees of uncertainty

20. In an agile/adaptive environment project that has high variability but must also hold to a strict budget, what approach should the project manager take to stay within the cost constraints?

A. Adjust the scope and schedule.

B. Reduce staffing.

C. Expand the project schedule.

D. Reduce the project schedule.

21. Which of the following is the correct formula to use when calculating Variance at Completion (VAC)?

A. EAC – AC

B. BAC – EAC

C. EV / AC

D. EV – PV

22. Which value for CV indicates that the project is over budget?

A. CV = 0

B. CV > 0

C. CV < 0

D. CV = 1

23. Which CPI measurement indicates that the project is currently experiencing a cost underrun?

    A. CPI = 1.2

    B. CPI = 0.8

    C. CPI = 1

    D. CPI = 0

24. Your current project has a planned value of 30, earned value of 35, and an actual value of 28. Which of the following values can be derived?

    A. SPI = 0.86

    B. SV = -5

    C. CPI = 1.25

    D. CV = -7

25. Your project has a dependency on an outside contractor and that contractor has fallen behind schedule. The contractor is promising to make up the ground lost and complete on their original deadline. You have calculated the following values for the current point in time: BAC = $12,000, PV = $8,000, EV = $7,000, AC = 9,000, SPI = 0.87, and CPI = 0.77. In order for the contractor to meet the original plan, what level of efficiency must the contractor maintain for the remainder of the project?

    A. 60%

    B. 80%

    C. -133%

    D. 167%

26. The expenses for your project are consistently showing the same CPI for each month of the project completed so far, and there are two months left in the project. Which formula should you use to calculate the project's estimate at completion?

    A. AC + ETC

    B. BAC / CPI

    C. AC + (Remaining PV / CPI)

    D. AC + BAC - EV

27. Your current project was originally estimated to cost $1.5 million with a completion target of six months. You are three months into the project and have performed an earned value analysis with the following results: EV = $650,000, PV = $750,000, and AC = $800,000. What are the schedule and cost variances?

    A. SV = $100,000 / CV = $150,000

    B. SV = $150,000 / CV = -$100,000

    C. SV = -$50,000 / CV = $150,000

    D. SV = -$100,000 / CV = -$150,000

1. C	**10.** B	**19.** D
2. C	**11.** A	**20.** A
3. D	**12.** C	**21.** B
4. B	**13.** D	**22.** C
5. C	**14.** C	**23.** A
6. C	**15.** B	**24.** C
7. D	**16.** A	**25.** D
8. A	**17.** C	**26.** B
9. B	**18.** D	**27.** D

1. Which of the following are often closely linked, particularly on smaller projects?

    A. Collecting requirements and testing product

    B. Planning the project and closing the project

    C. Cost estimating and cost budgeting

    D. Developing the team and managing the team

    ☑ **C.** On small projects, estimating and budgeting costs are often done simultaneously and therefore are very closely linked and are often viewed as a single process carried out in a short period of time.

    ☒ **A, B,** and **D** are incorrect because all are closely linked on all projects, including small projects. **A** is incorrect because collecting requirements and testing the product are linked on all projects because tests need to show the fulfillment of the requirements. **B** is incorrect because planning the project and closing the project are linked because a project manager cannot close a project unless all planned objectives have been met. **D** is incorrect because spending time as a project manager to develop a team and manage a team are important on every project and are closely linked.

2. In which process does the project manager aggregate the estimated costs of individual activities in order to establish a cost baseline?

    A. Plan Cost Management

    B. Estimate Costs

    C. Determine Budget

    D. Control Costs

    ☑ **C.** The Project Cost Management process of the Determine Budget process is where the project manager summarizes the costs that were estimated for each individual activity in order to create the cost baseline for the project.

    ☒ **A, B,** and **D** are incorrect. It is in the Determine Budget process (not Plan Cost Management, Estimate Costs, or Control Costs process) that the project manager summarizes the costs that were estimated for each individual activity in order to create the cost baseline for the project.

3. What is the key benefit of the Plan Cost Management process?

    A. Provides estimates for project costs at the beginning of the project

    B. Provides summary information to review project costs at the end of the project

    C. Provides ratios and variance analysis results reviewed at the end of the project

    D. Provides guidance on how project costs will be managed throughout the project

☑ **D.** The Plan Cost Management process provides direction and guidance throughout the project on how costs will be managed. As a planning process, consideration of the project cost particulars includes deciding how to estimate the costs, how to budget the costs, how to manage the costs, and how to monitor and control the costs. The work including these tasks is not a planning process but is instead an Executing and Monitoring and Controlling process.

☒ **A**, **B**, and **C** are incorrect. **A** is incorrect because although estimates can be planned at the beginning of the project, they may also be planned at predefined points in the project. **B** is incorrect because the Plan Cost Management process does not create summary information for review at the end of the project; instead, it happens early and at predefined points during the project. **C** is incorrect because the calculation of ratios and derivation of variances is done as a part of the Control Costs process.

4. Which process creates an approximate monetary value for each project activity necessary to complete the work of the project?

   A. Plan Cost Management

   B. Estimate Costs

   C. Determine Budget

   D. Control Costs

   ☑ **B.** In the Project Cost Management process Estimate Costs, the project manager establishes estimates of the approximate amount of money needed to complete each activity in the project. A variety of estimation techniques (analogous, parametric, bottom-up, etc.) are used to estimate activity costs.

   ☒ **A**, **C**, and **D** are incorrect. **A** is incorrect because Plan Cost Management is about planning and choosing which estimation techniques to use to estimate costs. **C** is incorrect because Determine Budget is done after Estimate Costs and makes use of the estimates for activities in order to create an overall project budget. **D** is incorrect because in the Control Costs process, the project manager compares planned costs to actual costs and takes corrective action if variances are found.

5. What process are you performing if you are adding together the costs of individual activities into work packages and then rolling the work packages into control accounts and finishing with summarizing the control accounts?

   A. Plan Cost Management

   B. Estimate Costs

   C. Determine Budget

   D. Control Costs

   ☑ **C.** Aggregating activity estimates for work packages, which is what you are performing in this question, is a part of the Determine Budget process. Aggregates are created for the work packages level, then into the control account level, and finishing with the overall summary for the project budget.

⊠ **A**, **B**, and **D** are incorrect. **A** is incorrect because Plan Cost Management is about planning and choosing how to estimate, budget, and control costs during the project. **B** is incorrect because in the Estimate Costs process, the project manager establishes estimates of the approximate amount of money needed to complete all project activities. **D** is incorrect because in the Control Costs process, the project manager compares planned costs to actual costs and takes corrective action if variances are found.

6. In which process does the project manager perform a reserve analysis to account for unknown-unknown risks?

    A. Plan Cost Management

    B. Estimate Costs

    C. Determine Budget

    D. Control Costs

☑ **C.** In the Determine Budget process, the project manager performs a reserve analysis to account for management reserves and contingency reserves in the project budget and project schedule. Time and money are set aside to handle unknown-unknown risks as a part of management reserves.

⊠ **A**, **B**, and **D** are incorrect. **A** is incorrect because Plan Cost Management is about planning and choosing how to estimate, budget, and control project costs during the project. **B** is incorrect because in the Estimate Costs process, the project manager establishes estimates of the approximate amount of money needed to complete all project activities. **D** is incorrect because in the Control Costs process, the project manager compares planned costs to actual costs and takes corrective action if variances are found.

7. In which process is the project manager performing a variance analysis in order to take any necessary corrective actions to realign the project work with the project budget?

    A. Plan Cost Management

    B. Estimate Costs

    C. Determine Budget

    D. Control Costs

☑ **D.** In the Control Costs process, the project manager performs a variance analysis of costs and schedules, comparing what was planned to what is actually happening. A project manager takes corrective action if variances are found in order to realign the project work with the project budget and project schedule, making adjustments to the work, the budget, and the schedule if necessary.

⊠ **A**, **B**, and **C** are incorrect. **A** is incorrect because Plan Cost Management is about planning and choosing how to estimate, budget, and control project costs during the project. **B** is incorrect because in the Estimate Costs process, the project manager establishes estimates of the approximate amount of money needed to complete all project activities. **C** is incorrect because Determine Budget is done after Estimate Costs and makes use of the estimates for activities in order to create an overall project budget.

8. During project planning, you notice you do not have much information about one activity. You decide to estimate activity duration by referring to the actual duration of a similar activity on another project. This calculation method is called:

   A. Analogous estimating

   B. Expert judgment

   C. Parametric estimating

   D. Reserve analysis

   ☑ A. Estimating the duration of a project activity by referring to the actual duration of a similar activity on another project is known as analogous estimating.

   ☒ B, C, and D are incorrect. B is incorrect because expert judgment uses the opinions of specialists combined with their historical experience. C is incorrect because parametric estimating uses variables (e.g., $10 per square foot to install carpet) or metrics to calculate an estimate. D is incorrect because reserve analysis refers to contingency or time buffers, not estimating time and cost.

9. Which technique are you using if you are calculating the theoretical early start and finish dates on your project schedule, along with late start and finish dates, for all the project activities?

   A. Critical chain method

   B. Critical path method

   C. Schedule compression

   D. What-if analysis

   ☑ B. Calculating the theoretical early start and finish dates, along with late start and finish dates, for all of the project activities using a forward and backward pass analysis is known as the critical path method.

   ☒ A, C, and D are incorrect. A is incorrect because the critical chain method is specifically related to resource constraints. C is incorrect because schedule compression is about reducing project duration. D is incorrect because what-if analysis relates to calculating the durations of multiple combinations of tasks based on possible scenarios.

10. Your project sponsor for the current project expects to receive a narrow estimate for project costs because all project information is now known. Which of the following is considered a suitable range for this request?

    A. −100% to +100%

    B. −10% to +10%

    C. −25% to +25%

    D. −50% to +50%

    ☑ B. It represents the smallest or narrowest range of percentages present in the answers. With all information known for the project, usually later in a project, a project manager can create their best estimates within a narrow range.

☒ **A, C,** and **D** are incorrect because all of these answers offer wider ranges than +/–10%. Early in a project—for example, in the initiation stage when there is still information that needs to be progressively elaborated—estimates usually have a larger range.

11. You are calculating costs for your project based on costs from a previous similar project that was completed last month in your organization. This process is known as:

    A. Analogous estimating

    B. Bottom-up estimating

    C. Parametric estimating

    D. Three-point estimating

    ☑ **A.** Using costs from a previous similar project that has been completed in your organization is known as analogous estimating.

    ☒ **B, C,** and **D** are incorrect. **B** is incorrect because bottom-up estimating is based on WBS activities, with values provided for each task. **C** is incorrect because parametric estimating is based on pro-rata calculations from standard rates using a rate as an input parameter to a calculation. **D** is incorrect because three-point estimating requires three data points rather than similar project data.

12. What estimation technique is your builder using if the cost has been presented to you as $100 per square foot?

    A. Analogous estimating

    B. Bottom-up estimating

    C. Parametric estimating

    D. Three-point estimating

    ☑ **C.** Parametric estimating is based on pro-rata calculations from standard rates based on a mathematical model using a rate, or metric, as an input parameter to a calculation.

    ☒ **A, B,** and **D** are incorrect. **A** is incorrect because using costs from a previous similar project that has been completed in the organization is known as analogous estimating. **B** is incorrect because bottom-up estimating is based on WBS activities and aggregating to create the project estimate. **D** is incorrect because three-point estimating requires three data points, and the question does not provide evidence of the three data points (optimistic, pessimistic, most likely).

13. Which estimation technique can make use of either triangular distribution or beta distribution?

    A. Analogous estimating

    B. Bottom-up estimating

    C. Parametric estimating

    D. Three-point estimating

☑ **D.** Three-point estimating is commonly performed using either the triangular distribution formula of (Optimistic + Most Likely + Pessimistic) / 3 or the beta distribution formula of (Optimistic + (4 * Most Likely) + Pessimistic) / 6. The beta distribution weights the most likely possibility with a higher probability by multiplying by 4.

☒ **A**, **B**, and **C** are incorrect. Analogous, bottom-up, and parametric estimating do not make use of the triangular distribution or beta distribution formula.

14. Given a most likely value of 12, an optimistic value of 10, and a pessimistic value of 20, using the triangular distribution formula, what is the estimate for the task?

   A. 7

   B. 13

   C. 14

   D. 26

   ☑ **C.** The formula for three-point estimation using a triangular distribution is (Optimistic + Most Likely + Pessimistic) / 3, with no additional weight given to the most likely value, yielding (12 + 10 + 20) / 3 = 14.

   ☒ **A**, **B**, and **D** are incorrect. **A** is incorrect because the formula for three-point estimation using a triangular distribution is (Optimistic + Most Likely + Pessimistic) / 3 with no additional weight given to the most likely value. The incorrect formula used to reach the value of 7 is (12 + 10 + 20) / 6. **B** is incorrect because the beta distribution formula was used to reach the value of 13, giving the most likely value additional weight: ((4 * 12) + 10 + 20) / 6 = 13. **D** is incorrect because the formula used to reach the value of 26 is ((4 * 12) + 10 + 20) / 3 = 26.

15. Which process group are you carrying out if you are primarily concerned with ensuring the project has the funds necessary for the resources needed to complete the project work?

   A. Project Scope Management

   B. Project Cost Management

   C. Project Resource Management

   D. Project Stakeholder Management

   ☑ **B.** The process group of Project Cost Management is primarily concerned with the cost of the resources needed to complete project activities.

   ☒ **A**, **C**, and **D** are incorrect. **A** is incorrect because Project Scope Management is primarily concerned with identifying and controlling what work is done during a project, not its cost. **C** is incorrect because Project Resource Management is primarily concerned with identifying, acquiring, and managing the human and physical resources of the project. **D** is incorrect because Project Stakeholder Management is primarily concerned with identifying and engaging stakeholders throughout the project.

16. Which concern is being highlighted if the cost of an acquired item is allowed to be measured when the acquisition decision is made versus when the order is placed, versus when the item is delivered, versus when the actual cost is incurred?

A. Different stakeholders measure project costs in different ways and at different times.

B. Costs for a project cannot be accurately predicted.

C. Project costs should have multiple values associated with each line item.

D. Use multiple methods to measure costs and then aggregate all measurements.

☑ **A.** Cost decisions introduced into a given project can vary based on how different projects choose to measure project cost. In many organizations, this variability is addressed by standardizing financial performance measures outside of all projects, for instance, by having a program management office (PMO) standardize the way costs will be calculated for all projects in the organization.

☒ **B, C,** and **D** are incorrect. **B** is incorrect because costs for a project can be accurately predicted given an agreed-upon approach for all projects. **C** is incorrect because project costs should have a single value associated with each line item. **D** is incorrect because using multiple methods to measure costs and then aggregating all measurements is not standard practice and will lead to an inability to compare costs across projects.

17. What is the trend in Project Cost Management called Earned Schedules (ES) theory?

A. Replaces the cost variance measure of Earned Value (EV) minus Planned Value (PV) with Earned Schedules (ES) minus Actual Time (AT)

B. Replaces the cost variance measure of Earned Value (EV) plus Planned Value (PV) with Earned Schedules (ES) plus Actual Time (AT)

C. Replaces the schedule variance measure of Earned Value (EV) minus Planned Value (PV) with Earned Schedules (ES) minus Actual Time (AT)

D. Replaces the schedule variance measure of Earned Value (EV) plus Planned Value (PV) with Earned Schedules (ES) plus Actual Time (AT)

☑ **C.** An emerging trend within the Project Cost Management process is to replace the schedule variance calculation with an earned schedule calculation. For schedule variance, the calculation is SV = EV – PV (Earned Value minus Planned Value). Under the theory of Earned Schedules, the replacement calculation is SV = ES – AT (Earned Schedules minus Actual Time).

☒ **A, B,** and **D** are incorrect. **A** and **B** are incorrect because both answers focus on cost, not schedules. **D** is incorrect because the statement uses "plus" instead of "minus."

18. If your organization does not have an existing formal or informal cost estimation approach in place, what should you do as the project manager as a part of Project Cost Management?

    A. Set a zero budget at the start of Project Cost Management and add costs to the budget as the project is progressively elaborated.

    B. Transfer the responsibility for Project Cost Management to the PMO.

    C. Set a budget that equals that of the previous project and update throughout the project.

    D. Tailor the way Project Cost Management processes are applied.

    ☑ **D.** One of the tailoring considerations a project manager should consider is modifying how the Project Cost Management processes are applied if there is no pre-existing way (formal or informal) of performing cost estimation in the organization.

    ☒ **A**, **B**, and **C** are incorrect. **A** is incorrect because setting a zero budget as the start of the Project Cost Management process and adding costs to it during the project is not considered estimating or budgeting. **B** is incorrect because it is unlikely there is a PMO for the organization. If there is a PMO, standards for how to estimate costs and develop project budgets would exist. **C** is incorrect because using a budget that equals that of the previous project will only be valid if all other project variables are the same. Regardless, a budget is not updated throughout the project.

19. When should a project manager make use of lightweight estimation methods to generate a high-level forecast of project labor costs?

    A. On large projects

    B. On small projects

    C. On projects where the scope is fully defined

    D. On projects with high degrees of uncertainty

    ☑ **D.** Projects with high degrees of uncertainty or those where the scope is not yet fully defined may not benefit from detailed cost calculations due to the high frequency of changes. This is typically seen in agile/adaptive environments.

    ☒ **A**, **B**, and **C** are incorrect. **A** and **B** are incorrect because the decision to use a lightweight estimation method to forecast project labor costs is not related to the size of the project. **C** is incorrect because if the scope is fully defined, accurate and complete estimates can be made, meaning lightweight estimates are not appropriate.

20. In an agile/adaptive environment project that has high variability but must also hold to a strict budget, what approach should the project manager take to stay within the cost constraints?

    A. Adjust the scope and schedule.

    B. Reduce staffing.

    C. Expand the project schedule.

    D. Reduce the project schedule.

☑ **A.** If a high-variability agile/adaptive project must also hold to a strict budget, the project manager can adjust the project scope and project schedule to stay within budget.

☒ **B, C,** and **D** are incorrect. **B** is incorrect because reducing staff on the project may not address the project cost. For example, if two people could accomplish the work in one month, it will now take one person two months netting the same project cost. **C** and **D** are incorrect because expanding or reducing the project schedule by itself is unlikely to fully address the project cost.

21. Which of the following is the correct formula to use when calculating Variance at Completion (VAC)?

    A. EAC – AC

    B. BAC – EAC

    C. EV / AC

    D. EV – PV

    ☑ **B.** Variance at Completion (VAC) equals Budget at Completion (BAC) minus Estimate at Completion (EAC). It is important to know the words associated with the acronym in addition to understanding what the calculation tells you about the project. VAC predicts the project overrun (negative VAC) or project underrun (positive VAC).

    ☒ **A, C,** and **D** are incorrect. **A** is incorrect because Estimate at Completion (EAC) minus Actual Cost (AC) is the formula for Estimate to Completion (ETC). **C** is incorrect because Earned Value (EV) divided by Actual Cost (AC) is the formula for Cost Performance Index (CPI). **D** is incorrect because Earned Value (EV) minus Planned Value (PV) is the formula for Cost Variance (CV).

22. Which value for CV indicates that the project is over budget?

    A. CV = 0

    B. CV > 0

    C. CV < 0

    D. CV = 1

    ☑ **C.** For variance analysis, negative values are bad and positive values are good. When CV = 0, the project is on budget. When CV > 0, the project is within budget. When CV < 0, the project is over budget.

    ☒ **A, B,** and **D** are incorrect. For variance analysis, negative values are bad news and positive values are good news. **A** is incorrect because a project is on budget when CV = 0. **B** is incorrect because a project is under budget when CV > 0. **D** is incorrect because when the CV = 1, which is greater than zero, the project is under budget.

23. Which CPI measurement indicates that the project is currently experiencing a cost underrun?

    A. CPI = 1.2

    B. CPI = 0.8

    C. CPI = 1

    D. CPI = 0

    ☑ **A.** The cost performance index measures the cost efficiency of budgeted resources as a ratio of earned value to actual cost. A CPI of greater than 1 indicates a cost underrun of performance to date. CPI is calculated using CPI = EV / AC.

    ☒ **B, C,** and **D** are incorrect. **B** and **D** are incorrect because a CPI of less than 1 indicates a cost overrun for work completed to date; both 0.8 and 0 are less than 1. **C** is incorrect because a CPI of 0 indicates the project is exactly on track for cost efficiency and is not running over or under the earned value to date as compared to actual cost.

24. Your current project has a planned value of 30, earned value of 35, and an actual value of 28. Which of the following values can be derived?

    A. SPI = 0.86

    B. SV = –5

    C. CPI = 1.25

    D. CV = –7

    ☑ **C.** Using the formula of CPI = EV / AC yields the value 1.25; the cost performance index measures the cost efficiency of budgeted resources as a ratio of earned value to actual cost. The earned value is 35; the actual cost is 28.

    ☒ **A, B,** and **D** are incorrect. **A** is incorrect because SPI = EV / PV; therefore, using the values provided, SPI would be 35 / 30, equaling 1.17, not 0.86; 0.86 was arrived at by incorrectly using PV / EV. **B** is incorrect because SV is calculated using SV = EV – PV, which would be 35 – 30, equaling 5, not –5. **D** is incorrect because CV is calculated using CV = EV – AC, which would be 35 – 28, equaling 7; incorrectly applying the formula as AC – EV would give the answer of –7.

25. Your project has a dependency on an outside contractor and that contractor has fallen behind schedule. The contractor is promising to make up the ground lost and complete on their original deadline. You have calculated the following values for the current point in time: BAC = $12,000, PV = $8,000, EV = $7,000, AC = 9,000, SPI = 0.87, and CPI = 0.77. In order for the contractor to meet the original plan, what level of efficiency must the contractor maintain for the remainder of the project?

    A. 60%

    B. 80%

    C. –133%

    D. 167%

☑ **D.** Total complete performance index (TCPI) is the estimate of the future cost performance needed to complete the project as originally planned and is calculated using the formula TCPI = (BAC − EV) / (BAC − AC). SPI and CPI are extraneous information for this question. ($12,000 − $7,000) / ($12,000 − $9,000) = 1.67 (TCPI = 167%).

☒ **A, B,** and **C** are incorrect. The formula TCPI = (BAC − EV) / (BAC − AC) is used to calculate the efficiency that must be maintained to complete on time. SPI and CPI are extraneous information for this question.

26. The expenses for your project are consistently showing the same CPI for each month of the project completed so far, and there are two months left in the project. Which formula should you use to calculate the project's estimate at completion?

   A. AC + ETC

   B. BAC / CPI

   C. AC + (Remaining PV / CPI)

   D. AC + BAC − EV

   ☑ **B.** When variances are typical of future variances, which is what the next two months of the project represent, you should calculate the project's estimate at completion by using the formula EAC = BAC / CPI.

   ☒ **A, C,** and **D** are incorrect. **A** is incorrect because AC (Actual Cost) + ETC (Estimate to Complete) is a made-up formula. **C** is incorrect because it is a made-up formula. **D** is incorrect because it is the formula for calculating EAC if the future work will be accomplished at the planned rate.

27. Your current project was originally estimated to cost $1.5 million with a completion target of six months. You are three months into the project and have performed an earned value analysis with the following results: EV = $650,000, PV = $750,000, and AC = $800,000. What are the schedule and cost variances?

   A. SV = $100,000 / CV = $150,000

   B. SV = $150,000 / CV = −$100,000

   C. SV = −$50,000 / CV = $150,000

   D. SV = −$100,000 / CV = −$150,000

   ☑ **D.** Using the values provided and the formulas for schedule and cost variances of SV = EV − PV and CV = EV − AC, SV= −$100,000 and CV= −$150,000.

   ☒ **A, B,** and **C** are incorrect. These answers do not come from using the numbers provided in the correct formulas. Using the values provided and the formulas for schedule and cost variances of SV = EV − PV and CV = EV − AC, SV= −$100,000 and CV= −$150,000.

CHAPTER 8

Project Quality Management

In this chapter, you will

- Understand the three project management processes in the Project Quality Management knowledge area
- Identify the input, tools, techniques and outputs defined in the three quality management processes
- Understand the reasons for and approaches to adapting quality management in different project environments

The Project Quality Management knowledge area accounts for 7 percent (21) of the questions on the CAPM exam. The *PMBOK Guide, Sixth Edition*, Sections 8.1 through 8.3, cover the three processes in the Project Quality Management knowledge area.

This chapter focuses on the topic of Project Quality Management. Project Quality Management, like the other knowledge areas, begins with a process of planning that produces a quality management plan. It then has an executing process, Manage Quality, which is focused on defining and checking the quality of the processes in the project. It also has a monitoring and controlling process, Control Quality, which is focused upon defining and inspecting the quality of the project deliverables.

You may need to pay attention in this chapter to those activities and the range of different quality tools that are described, because many of them may be new to you.

The 21 practice questions in this chapter are mapped to the style and frequency of question types you will see on the CAPM exam.

1. What are the three processes in the Quality Management knowledge area?

    A. Control Quality, Manage Quality, Plan Quality Management

    B. Plan Quality Management, Control Assurance, Perform Quality Control

    C. Perform Quality Control, Determine Quality, Plan Quality Management

    D. Plan Quality Management, Assure Quality, Control Quality

2. Which of the following is not one of the data representation techniques used in the Project Quality Management knowledge area?

    A. Checklists

    B. Scatter diagrams

    C. Control chart

    D. Affinity diagram

3. What does it mean if a single data point appears above the upper specification limit on a control chart?

    A. The process is in control and the customer is happy.

    B. The process may be out of control, and consideration should be given to checking the process soon.

    C. A single data point outside the upper specification is okay. You only need to be concerned if there are seven consecutive data points outside either of the specification limits.

    D. The process is out of control and requires immediate action, because the customer will not accept any deliverables outside the specification limit.

4. What is the best definition of quality?

    A. Quality is whatever the customer says is right.

    B. Quality is the degree to which a product can be used for its intended purpose.

    C. Quality is the degree to which a set of inherent characteristics fulfills requirements.

    D. Quality is the number of features that the product has.

5. What is the best definition of the principle of Kaizen?

    A. Defining quality processes and checking that they are being used

    B. Continuously improving

    C. Checking the quality of the product

    D. Having a quality management plan

6. If you are considering the impact of potential future warranty claims as part of your quality management plan, what are you considering?

   A. Cost of quality

   B. Quality assurance

   C. Benchmarking

   D. Prevention over inspection

7. If you are using a diagram to determine the potential causes of quality issues, what would you be using?

   A. Control chart

   B. Histogram

   C. Checksheet

   D. Fishbone diagram

8. If you are testing and measuring a small sample and extrapolating those results to be indicative of a total population, what tool or technique are you using?

   A. Benchmarking

   B. Statistical sampling

   C. Design of experiments

   D. Brainstorming

9. If you are conducting an audit to check whether processes are being followed correctly, what process are you involved in?

   A. Plan Quality Management

   B. Control Quality

   C. Manage Quality

   D. Perform Quality Audit

10. What are the variables and allowable variations called that should be measured as part of the Manage Quality and Control Quality processes?

    A. Quality control measurements

    B. Quality checklists

    C. Quality metrics

    D. Cost of quality

11. Which quality process uses inspection as a tool or technique?

   A. Plan Quality Management

   B. Control Quality

   C. Manage Quality

   D. Perform Quality Inspection

12. Translating the quality management plan into executable quality activities during the execution phase is:

   A. Execute Quality Management

   B. Manage Quality

   C. Control Quality

   D. Project Quality Management

13. A structured, independent process to determine whether project activities comply with project policies, processes, and procedures is called a:

   A. Quality inspection

   B. Quality audit

   C. Retrospective

   D. Quality demo

14. You are translating the quality management plan into executable quality activities. Which of the following inputs will be least helpful to you?

   A. Quality control measurements

   B. Process improvement plan

   C. Lessons learned register

   D. Risk report

15. Two of the common quality improvement tools are:

   A. Define, Measure, Analyze, Improve, and Control (DMAIC) and three-point estimating

   B. Design of experiments (DOE) and mean time between failures (MTBF)

   C. Logical data models and suppliers, inputs, process, outputs, and customers (SIPOC)

   D. Plan–do–check–act (PDCA) and Six Sigma

16. Which of the following is least useful as an input for managing quality?

   A. Quality control measurements

   B. Quality metrics

   C. Risk report

   D. Resource capabilities and availability

17. Which of the following is least useful as an input for performing the Manage Quality process?

    A. Quality management plan

    B. Quality metrics

    C. Resource availability

    D. Lessons learned register

18. Which project management processes in the Executing process group provide change requests as an input to the Perform Integrated Change Control process?

    A. Direct and Manage Project Execution, Schedule Control

    B. Manage Quality, Project Contract Administration

    C. Direct and Manage Project Work, Perform Quality Control

    D. Implement Risk Responses, Manage Quality, Direct and Manage Project Work

19. Which of the following is an input to the Manage Quality process?

    A. Quality metrics

    B. Project requirements

    C. Change requests

    D. Validated deliverables

20. A project manager is trying to identify the best project practices being used and gaps between best practices and current practices, as well as sharing the best practices introduced or implemented in similar projects in the organization. This is known as:

    A. Developing the quality metrics

    B. Performing a quality audit

    C. Setting the quality baseline

    D. Building quality checklists

21. Recommending corrective actions to increase the effectiveness and efficiency of the organization falls under the Manage Quality process ITTOs (inputs, tools and techniques, and outputs). This list of actions is documented as:

    A. Change requests

    B. Organizational process asset (OPA) updates

    C. Project management plan updates

    D. Recommended preventive actions

1. A	**8.** B	**15.** D
2. A	**9.** C	**16.** D
3. D	**10.** C	**17.** C
4. C	**11.** B	**18.** D
5. B	**12.** B	**19.** A
6. A	**13.** B	**20.** B
7. D	**14.** B	**21.** C

1. What are the three processes in the Quality Management knowledge area?

   A. Control Quality, Manage Quality, Plan Quality Management

   B. Plan Quality Management, Control Assurance, Perform Quality Control

   C. Perform Quality Control, Determine Quality, Plan Quality Management

   D. Plan Quality Management, Assure Quality, Control Quality

   ☑ **A.** The three processes in the Quality Management knowledge area are Plan Quality Management, Manage Quality, and Control Quality.

   ☒ **B**, **C**, and **D** are incorrect. **B** is incorrect because there is no process called Control Assurance. **C** is incorrect because there is no process called Perform Quality Control or Determine Quality. **D** is incorrect because there is no process called Assure Quality.

2. Which of the following is not one of the data representation techniques used in the Project Quality Management knowledge area?

   A. Checklists

   B. Scatter diagrams

   C. Control chart

   D. Affinity diagram

   ☑ **A.** Checklists are a data-gathering technique not a data representation technique.

   ☒ **B**, **C**, and **D** are incorrect. **B** is incorrect because the scatter diagram is one of the data representation techniques used in the Control Quality process. **C** is incorrect because control charts are a data representation technique used in the Control Quality process. **D** is incorrect because affinity diagrams are a data representation technique used in the Manage Quality process.

3. What does it mean if a single data point appears above the upper specification limit on a control chart?

   A. The process is in control and the customer is happy.

   B. The process may be out of control, and consideration should be given to checking the process soon.

   C. A single data point outside the upper specification is okay. You only need to be concerned if there are seven consecutive data points outside either of the specification limits.

   D. The process is out of control and requires immediate action, because the customer will not accept any deliverables outside the specification limit.

   ☑ **D.** Any data point outside the specification limits indicates that the process is out of control and should be investigated immediately.

☒ **A**, **B**, and **C** are incorrect. **A** is incorrect because a data point outside the specification limit does not mean that the process is in control; the customer will not pay for anything that is outside the specification limit. **B** is incorrect because a data point outside the specification limit indicates that the process is out of control and should be investigated immediately. **C** is incorrect because a single data point outside the specification limit indicates that something is wrong. The rule of seven applies to consecutive data points within the control limits.

4. What is the best definition of quality?

   A. Quality is whatever the customer says is right.

   B. Quality is the degree to which a product can be used for its intended purpose.

   C. Quality is the degree to which a set of inherent characteristics fulfills requirements.

   D. Quality is the number of features that the product has.

   ☑ **C.** Quality is the degree to which a set of inherent characteristics fulfills requirements—remember this definition for the exam.

   ☒ **A**, **B**, and **D** are incorrect. **A** is incorrect because quality doesn't necessarily relate to what the customer says is right, unless what the customer says is right is captured in the requirements. **B** is incorrect because quality is more than the degree to which a product can be used for its intended purpose. **D** is incorrect because the amount of features a product has, or does not have, refers to grade, not quality.

5. What is the best definition of the principle of Kaizen?

   A. Defining quality processes and checking that they are being used

   B. Continuously improving

   C. Checking the quality of the product

   D. Having a quality management plan

   ☑ **B.** Kaizen is the loose Japanese translation of the term *continuously improving.*

   ☒ **A**, **C**, and **D** are incorrect. **A** is incorrect because defining quality processes and checking that they are being used is the process of Quality Assurance. **C** is incorrect because checking the quality of the product is the process of Quality Control. **D** is incorrect because having a quality management plan is the process of Planning Quality Management.

6. If you are considering the impact of potential future warranty claims as part of your quality management plan, what are you considering?

   A. Cost of quality

   B. Quality assurance

   C. Benchmarking

   D. Prevention over inspection

☑ **A.** Cost of quality, mirrored by the cost of low quality, considers the impacts of quality decisions over the entire life of the product.

☒ **B, C,** and **D** are incorrect. **B** is incorrect because quality assurance is the process of defining processes and checking that you are using them as planned. **C** is incorrect because benchmarking is the process of comparing your efforts against other projects or organizations. **D** is incorrect because prevention over inspection is a key concept of the overall approach to Project Quality Management.

7. If you are using a diagram to determine the potential causes of quality issues, what would you be using?

   A. Control chart

   B. Histogram

   C. Checksheet

   D. Fishbone diagram

   ☑ **D.** A fishbone diagram, also called an Ishikawa diagram or cause-and-effect diagram, shows a graphical representation of potential causes of an event.

   ☒ **A, B,** and **C** are incorrect. **A** is incorrect because a control chart maps data points against an expected mean; upper and lower control limits set three standard deviations either side of the mean. **B** is incorrect because a histogram, or bar chart, is a graphical way of representing frequency or total occurrences of data. **C** is incorrect because a checksheet is a standardized description of processes, steps, and information to be completed or gathered.

8. If you are testing and measuring a small sample and extrapolating those results to be indicative of a total population, what tool or technique are you using?

   A. Benchmarking

   B. Statistical sampling

   C. Design of experiments

   D. Brainstorming

   ☑ **B.** Statistical sampling means taking a small sample of a total population for testing and then assuming those results apply to the entire population. It is used when there are simply too many tests to be done or when the testing involves destructive actions.

   ☒ **A, C,** and **D** are incorrect. **A** is incorrect because benchmarking is the process of comparing your efforts against other projects or organizations. **C** is incorrect because design of experiments (DOE) is the process of designing experiments to determine quality and considering the implications and effects upon the results. **D** is incorrect because brainstorming is a technique that gathers a group of people together and encourages them to think laterally about an issue.

9. If you are conducting an audit to check whether processes are being followed correctly, what process are you involved in?

    A. Plan Quality Management

    B. Control Quality

    C. Manage Quality

    D. Perform Quality Audit

    ☑ **C.** Manage Quality is the process of establishing processes and checking that you are following them by conducting audits.

    ☒ **A, B,** and **D** are incorrect. **A** is incorrect because Plan Quality Management is the initial planning process and delivers the quality management plan. **B** is incorrect because Control Quality uses inspection to determine the quality of the product. **D** is incorrect because Perform Quality Audit is a made-up process name.

10. What are the variables and allowable variations called that should be measured as part of the Manage Quality and Control Quality processes?

    A. Quality control measurements

    B. Quality checklists

    C. Quality metrics

    D. Cost of quality

    ☑ **C.** Quality metrics are defined during the Plan Quality Management process and set out the variables and allowable variations that should be measured as part of the Manage Quality and Control Quality processes.

    ☒ **A, B,** and **D** are incorrect. **A** is incorrect because quality control measurements are the measurements taken that allow you to assess whether quality metrics are being achieved. **B** is incorrect because a quality checklist is a standardized description of processes, steps, and information to be completed or gathered. **D** is incorrect because cost of quality considers the impact of quality decisions over the entire life of the product.

11. Which quality process uses inspection as a tool or technique?

    A. Plan Quality Management

    B. Control Quality

    C. Manage Quality

    D. Perform Quality Inspection

    ☑ **B.** The Control Quality process is focused on checking the quality of the product or deliverable and uses inspection as a tool.

⊠ **A**, **C**, and **D** are incorrect. **A** is incorrect because Plan Quality Management is the initial planning process and delivers the quality management plan. It does not use inspection as a tool or technique. **C** is incorrect because Manage Quality is the process of establishing processes and checking that you are following them by conducting audits. It does not use inspection as a tool or technique. **D** is incorrect because Quality Inspection is a made-up process name.

12. Translating the quality management plan into executable quality activities during the execution phase is:

    A. Execute Quality Management

    B. Manage Quality

    C. Control Quality

    D. Project Quality Management

    ☑ **B.** This is the definition of the Manage Quality process.

    ⊠ **A**, **C**, and **D** are incorrect. **A** is incorrect because Execute Quality Management is a made-up term. **C** is incorrect because Control Quality is a Monitoring and Controlling process group. **D** is incorrect because Project Quality Management is the name of a knowledge area.

13. A structured, independent process to determine whether project activities comply with project policies, processes, and procedures is called a:

    A. Quality inspection

    B. Quality audit

    C. Retrospective

    D. Quality demo

    ☑ **B.** This is the definition of a quality audit.

    ⊠ **A**, **C**, and **D** are incorrect. **A** is incorrect because a quality inspection involves reviewing the product to see if it meets the defined quality norms. Conducting reviews is an example of inspection. **C** is incorrect because at the end of each sprint, a sprint review meeting is held. During this meeting, the Scrum team shows what they accomplished during the sprint. Typically, this takes the form of a demo of the new features. A retrospective is the team's opportunity to examine their performance and capabilities to plan improvements for the next sprint. **D** is incorrect because at the end of each sprint, the team holds a sprint review meeting, where the team must demonstrate the user stories completed during the sprint to the product owner and other interested stakeholders.

14. You are translating the quality management plan into executable quality activities. Which of the following inputs will be least helpful to you?

    A. Quality control measurements

    B. Process improvement plan

    C. Lessons learned register

    D. Risk report

    ☑ **B.** The process improvement plan details the steps for analyzing project management and product development processes to identify activities that enhance their value.

    ☒ **A, C,** and **D** are incorrect. They are all inputs to the Manage Quality process.

15. Two of the common quality improvement tools are:

    A. Define, Measure, Analyze, Improve, and Control (DMAIC) and three-point estimating

    B. Design of experiments (DOE) and mean time between failures (MTBF)

    C. Logical data models and suppliers, inputs, process, outputs, and customers (SIPOC)

    D. Plan–do–check–act (PDCA) and Six Sigma

    ☑ **D.** Trends and emerging practices in Project Quality Management include PDCA, as defined by Shewhart and implemented by Deming. Six Sigma may improve project management processes and products.

    ☒ **A, B,** and **C** are incorrect. **A** is incorrect because DMAIC is an acronym for Define, Measure, Analyze, Improve, and Control and refers to a data-driven improvement cycle used for improving, optimizing, and stabilizing business processes and designs. The DMAIC improvement cycle is the core tool used to drive Six Sigma projects. The three-point estimating technique is used in estimating time and costs. **B** is incorrect because design of experiments (DOE) is a statistical method used in the Plan Quality process, and mean time between failures (MTBF) is a key performance indicator. **C** is incorrect because logical data models are used in data architecture to show a detailed representation of an organization's data, independent of any technology, and is described in business language; the SIPOC (supplier, input, process, output, customer) model is a type of flowchart used to map procedures.

16. Which of the following is least useful as an input for managing quality?

    A. Quality control measurements

    B. Quality metrics

    C. Risk report

    D. Resource capabilities and availability

    ☑ **D.** Resource capabilities and availability are not part of the input to managing quality.

☒ **A**, **B**, and **C** are incorrect. Each is part of the process of evaluating overall project performance on a regular basis to provide confidence that the project will comply with the relevant quality policies and standards. This is the Manage Quality process. Key inputs for this process include the quality management plan, quality control measurements, quality metrics, and the risk report.

17. Which of the following is least useful as an input for performing the Manage Quality process?

    A. Quality management plan

    B. Quality metrics

    C. Resource availability

    D. Lessons learned register

    ☑ **C.** Resource availability is not an input into the Manage Quality process.

    ☒ **A**, **B**, and **D** are incorrect. Each is part of the process of evaluating overall project performance on a regular basis to provide confidence that the project will comply with the relevant quality policies and standards, which are part of the Manage Quality process. Key inputs for this process include the quality management plan, quality metrics, and lessons learned register.

18. Which project management processes in the Executing process group provide change requests as an input to the Perform Integrated Change Control process?

    A. Direct and Manage Project Execution, Schedule Control

    B. Manage Quality, Project Contract Administration

    C. Direct and Manage Project Work, Perform Quality Control

    D. Implement Risk Responses, Manage Quality, Direct and Manage Project Work

    ☑ **D.** The Executing processes provide change requests as an input to the Perform Integrated Change Control processes of Implement Risk Responses, Manage Quality, and Direct and Manage Project Work.

    ☒ **A**, **B**, and **C** are incorrect. Each contains a variation of processes but not the exact inputs to the Perform Integrated Change Control process.

19. Which of the following is an input to the Manage Quality process?

    A. Quality metrics

    B. Project requirements

    C. Change requests

    D. Validated deliverables

    ☑ **A.** Quality metrics are an input to the Manage Quality process.

    ☒ **B**, **C**, and **D** are incorrect. **B** is incorrect because project requirements are not usually quality inputs. **C** is incorrect because change requests are an output of Manage Quality. **D** is incorrect because validated deliverables are an output of Control Quality.

20. A project manager is trying to identify the best project practices being used and gaps between best practices and current practices, as well as sharing the best practices introduced or implemented in similar projects in the organization. This is known as:

A. Developing the quality metrics

B. Performing a quality audit

C. Setting the quality baseline

D. Building quality checklists

☑ **B.** Identifying the good/best practices being implemented, identifying gaps/shortcomings, sharing the good practices introduced or implemented in similar projects in the organization and/or industry, proactively improving process implementation, and highlighting the results in the lessons learned repository is known as performing a quality audit.

☒ **A, C,** and **D** are incorrect. **A** is incorrect because quality metrics are an input to quality assurance and define the quality control measurements. **C** is incorrect because the quality baseline records the quality objectives for the project. **D** is incorrect because quality checklists are component specific.

21. Recommending corrective actions to increase the effectiveness and efficiency of the organization falls under the Manage Quality process ITTOs (inputs, tools and techniques, and outputs). This list of actions is documented as:

A. Change requests

B. Organizational process asset (OPA) updates

C. Project management plan updates

D. Recommended preventive actions

☑ **C.** Project management plan updates are related to changes to the quality management plan.

☒ **A, B,** and **D** are incorrect. **A** is incorrect because actions that have been recommended to increase the effectiveness and efficiency of the organization are documented as change requests. **B** is incorrect because process asset updates are changes to the processes. **D** is incorrect because change requests can be used to take corrective or preventive action, or to perform defect repair.

CHAPTER 9

Project Resource Management

In this chapter, you will

- Define the six project management processes in the Project Resource Management knowledge area
- Identify the inputs, tools, techniques, and outputs defined in the six processes in Project Resource Management
- Identify key concepts and trends in Project Resource Management, including tailoring and special considerations for agile/adaptive environments
- Identify techniques for developing a team, managing conflict, and resolving resource-related problems
- Understand the components of a resource management plan and data representation techniques for managing project resources

Every project needs resources, both human and physical. The art and science of managing project resources center on the project manager's ability to use a set of finite resources to create the deliverables that have been committed to through the project goals while remembering that a good portion of the resources are human beings that have needs of their own. The Project Resource Management process group contains six processes that focus on determining what resources a project needs, acquiring the resources, and then managing the acquired resources to the best advantage of the project. Certified Associate in Project Management (CAPM) candidates are tested on five objectives that emphasize the candidate's knowledge of acquiring and managing a team, as well as considering the planning needed to identify the human and physical resources required in a project.

The 24 practice questions in this chapter are mapped to the style and frequency of question types you will see on the CAPM exam.

1. Which process are you carrying out if you are deciding how to estimate time that will be needed by the quality testing group for the integrating testing phase of your project?

    A. Acquire Resources

    B. Control Resources

    C. Plan Resource Management

    D. Project Procurement Management

2. In which Project Resource Management process does a project manager compare the planned usage of a resource to its actual usage?

    A. Acquire Resources

    B. Control Resources

    C. Estimate Activity Resources

    D. Plan Resource Management

3. Which two processes take place during the Planning process group?

    A. Develop Project Charter and Identify Stakeholders

    B. Control Schedule and Control Costs

    C. Plan Resource Management and Estimate Activity Resources

    D. Direct and Manage Project Work and Acquire Resources

4. Which two processes require that a project manager know how to use techniques like expert judgment to create estimates?

    A. Plan Resource Management and Estimate Activity Resources

    B. Develop Team and Estimate Activity Resources

    C. Manage Team and Estimate Activity Resources

    D. Control Resources and Estimate Activity Resources

5. Which process in the Project Resource Management process group is concerned with tracking team member performance and resolving team issues?

    A. Acquire Resources

    B. Direct and Manage Work

    C. Develop Team

    D. Manage Team

6. One tool of project management is a table that identifies and describes the types and quantities of each resource required to complete all project work packages. What is this table known as?

    A. Resource calendar updates

    B. Activity attribute updates

    C. Resource breakdown structure

    D. Activity resource requirements

7. Which document is presented in a tabular form and includes the schedule milestones, documented assumptions and constraints, resource requirements by time period, and alternative schedules?

    A. Project schedule

    B. Schedule data

    C. Resource schedule

    D. Project bar chart

8. Which tool is a visual representation that illustrates the number of hours that each person will be needed each week over the course of the project schedule?

    A. Work breakdown structure

    B. Task network diagram

    C. Resource histogram

    D. Detailed Gantt chart

9. Which input to Plan Resource Management identifies the deliverables that drive the types and quantities of resources, which the project manager will need to manage?

    A. Quality management plan

    B. Resource management plan

    C. RACI chart

    D. Scope baseline

10. Which process creates the resource breakdown structure?

    A. Acquire Resources

    B. Control Resources

    C. Estimate Activity Resources

    D. Plan Resource Management

11. Which of the following is beneficial during the Planning phase in order to include relevant expertise and strengthen commitment to the project?

    A. The RACI chart

    B. Hiring an external consultant

    C. Identifying key performance indicators for requirements

    D. Participation of team members

12. As leader and manager of the project team, which of the following should the project manager be aware of as external project factors that may influence the project team?

    A. Names of the project sponsor and business analyst

    B. Quantitative and qualitative project risks

    C. Internal and external politics

    D. Business requirements and functional requirements

13. As the project manager, if you place an order for low-quality material in order to stay within the project budget, what is the exposure to the project or project team?

    A. There is risk that quality of the product may be compromised causing rework.

    B. There is a risk that deadlines may not be met.

    C. There is a risk that the project team will require training.

    D. There is a risk that the project sponsor will initiate a change request.

14. What are teams called that function with an absence of centralized control?

    A. Specialists

    B. Subject matter experts

    C. Self-organizing

    D. Self-sufficient

15. In a matrix management situation, which process is used to prevent unauthorized or conflicting assignments for team members between tasks for the functional manager and tasks for the project team?

    A. Monitor and Control Project Work

    B. Perform Integrated Change Control

    C. Control Resources

    D. Control Human Resources

16. Your company is undergoing a 12 percent reduction in workforce, and the project you are managing is affected. What should you do next?

    A. Carefully monitor and control the scarce resources.

    B. Request a preassigned contractor for needed resources.

    C. Suggest that a contracting officer representative (COR) be used for all project procurements.

    D. Use MoSCoW to reprioritize the work in your project.

17. Which estimation technique performs the estimation at the activity level and then aggregates up to develop estimates for work packages, control accounts, and summary project levels?

    A. Expert judgment

    B. Bottom-up estimating

C. Analogous estimating

D. Parametric estimating

18. Which process monitors and measures resources to ensure committed resources are made available and allocated according to the project management plan?

   A. Control Staffing

   B. Control Team

   C. Control Scope

   D. Control Resources

19. Your current project is in trouble per reports from the company's project steering committee, with many of the project issues stemming from a lack of resources. What should you do immediately?

   A. Tell the steering committee you have analyzed the work performance data, and the work performance reports are wrong.

   B. Start with general and background information about the project's performance.

   C. The problems from lack of resources have been noted in variance and trend analysis reports, which you are bringing to the project steering committee to justify more resources.

   D. You now need to re-baseline the project's schedule because of the resource shortage.

20. Which problem-solving technique focuses on achieving a win-win situation?

   A. Compromise/reconcile

   B. Collaborate/problem solve

   C. Force/direct

   D. Smooth/accommodate

21. Which data representation shows the company's existing departments, units, or teams together with project activities as work packages listed under each department?

   A. Hierarchical charts

   B. Work breakdown structure

   C. Organizational breakdown structure

   D. Resource breakdown structure

22. Which Project Resource Management group process uses multiple data representations as a technique for carrying out the process?

   A. Acquire Resources

   B. Control Resources

   C. Estimate Activity Resources

   D. Plan Resource Management

23. Given that multiple methods are available to document team member roles as a part of the Project Resource Management process, what are the shared objectives of all of the methods?

   A. Ensure each work package has an ambiguous owner.

   B. Ensure team members have a clear understanding of their roles and responsibilities.

   C. Create an organizational breakdown structure.

   D. Create a resource breakdown structure.

24. Which of the following will lead to the project manager tailoring the approach to Project Resource Management?

   A. Knowing whether the requirements will be captured with a formal or informal framework

   B. Identifying the risk threshold of the project sponsor

   C. Identifying the risk threshold of the project customer

   D. Knowing whether the team resources will be full-time or part-time

1. C	**9.** D	**17.** B
2. B	**10.** C	**18.** D
3. C	**11.** D	**19.** B
4. A	**12.** C	**20.** B
5. D	**13.** A	**21.** C
6. D	**14.** C	**22.** D
7. B	**15.** C	**23.** B
8. C	**16.** A	**24.** D

1. Which process are you carrying out if you are deciding how to estimate time that will be needed by the quality testing group for the integrating testing phase of your project?

   A. Acquire Resources

   B. Control Resources

   C. Plan Resource Management

   D. Project Procurement Management

   ☑ C. The Plan Resource Management process in the Project Resource Management process group is concerned with how to estimate, acquire, manage, and make use of both physical and team resources, which would include time with the quality testing group for integrating testing.

   ☒ A, B, and D are incorrect. A is incorrect because the Acquire Resources process in the Project Resource Management process group is the work to acquire; however, the question is asking about planning. B is incorrect because the Control Resources process in the Project Resource Management process group is about ensuring the assigned and allocated resources are available as planned in addition to monitoring usage versus planned. D is incorrect because Project Procurement Management is the process group concerned with creating acquisition relationships with vendors of goods and services external to the company.

2. In which Project Resource Management process does a project manager compare the planned usage of a resource to its actual usage?

   A. Acquire Resources

   B. Control Resources

   C. Estimate Activity Resources

   D. Plan Resource Management

   ☑ B. Monitoring the planned versus actual use of resources is done during Control Resources, and if there is a variance that needs to be corrected, corrective actions are taken as a part of Control Resources as well.

   ☒ A, C, and D are incorrect. A is incorrect because Acquire Resources is about obtaining human and physical resources for the project and happens before any actual usage information can be captured. C is incorrect because Estimate Activity Resources is about estimating time for team members as well as type and quantity for physical resources for the project, and this happens before any actual usage information can be captured. D is incorrect because Plan Resource Management precedes all other Project Resource Management process and well before any actual usage information can be captured.

3. Which two processes take place during the Planning process group?

   A. Develop Project Charter and Identify Stakeholders

   B. Control Schedule and Control Costs

C. Plan Resource Management and Estimate Activity Resources

D. Direct and Manage Project Work and Acquire Resources

☑ **C.** Both Plan Resource Management and Estimate Activity Resources take place as a part of the Planning Process Group.

☒ **A**, **B**, and **D** are incorrect. **A** is incorrect because Develop Project Charter and Identify Stakeholders are part of the Initiating Process Group. **B** is incorrect because Control Schedule and Control Costs are part of the Monitoring and Controlling process group. **D** is incorrect because Direct and Manage Project Work and Acquire Resources are part of the Executing Process Group.

4. Which two processes require that a project manager know how to use techniques like expert judgment to create estimates?

A. Plan Resource Management and Estimate Activity Resources

B. Develop Team and Estimate Activity Resources

C. Manage Team and Estimate Activity Resources

D. Control Resources and Estimate Activity Resources

☑ **A.** Both Plan Resource Management and Estimate Activity Resources require the project manager to use tools and techniques for estimation. Expert judgment includes past experiences and past projects and is a valuable tool used in both of these processes.

☒ **B**, **C**, and **D** are incorrect. **B** is incorrect because Develop Team does not use expert judgment or estimation. **C** is incorrect because Manage Team does not use expert judgment or estimation. **D** is incorrect because Control Resources does not use expert judgment or estimation.

5. Which process in the Project Resource Management process group is concerned with tracking team member performance and resolving team issues?

A. Acquire Resources

B. Direct and Manage Work

C. Develop Team

D. Manage Team

☑ **D.** The Manage Team process includes tracking team member performance, providing feedback to the team, helping to resolve issues, and managing any changes to the team to optimize project performance.

☒ **A**, **B**, and **C** are incorrect. **A** is incorrect because Acquire Resources is about obtaining the team members and is too early in the process to look at performance. **B** is incorrect because Direct and Manage Work is the executing process that directly carries out project work but does not look at team performance. **C** is incorrect because Develop Team focuses on improving competencies and team member interaction.

6. One tool of project management is a table that identifies and describes the types and quantities of each resource required to complete all project work packages. What is this table known as?

    A. Resource calendar updates

    B. Activity attribute updates

    C. Resource breakdown structure

    D. Activity resource requirements

    ☑ **D.** The set of activity resource requirements is a list that identifies and describes the types and quantities of each resource required to complete all project work packages.

    ☒ **A**, **B**, and **C** are incorrect. **A** and **B** are incorrect because although both are updates to outputs of the resource estimating activity, neither includes the types and quantities of each resource required to complete all project work packages. **C** is incorrect because the resource breakdown structure provides a decomposition of each resource for the project but does not include a type or quantity.

7. Which document is presented in a tabular form and includes the schedule milestones, documented assumptions and constraints, resource requirements by time period, and alternative schedules?

    A. Project schedule

    B. Schedule data

    C. Resource schedule

    D. Project bar chart

    ☑ **B.** The schedule data includes the schedule milestones, schedule activities, activity attributes, and documented assumptions and constraints, as well as resource requirements by time period, alternative schedules, and scheduling of contingency reserves.

    ☒ **A**, **C**, and **D** are incorrect. **A** is incorrect because the project schedule is a detail of activity start and end dates. **C** is incorrect because the resource schedule does not show weekends and vacations. **D** is incorrect because the project bar chart does not show the working days and shifts.

8. Which tool is a visual representation that illustrates the number of hours that each person will be needed each week over the course of the project schedule?

    A. Work breakdown structure

    B. Task network diagram

    C. Resource histogram

    D. Detailed Gantt chart

    ☑ **C.** A chart that illustrates the number of hours that each person will be needed each week over the course of the project schedule is known as a resource histogram.

⊠ **A**, **B**, and **D** are incorrect. **A** is incorrect because a WBS does not show weekly allocation. **B** is incorrect because a task network diagram is not used to show schedule information for resources. **D** is incorrect because a Gantt chart shows only task schedule information.

9. Which input to Plan Resource Management identifies the deliverables that drive the types and quantities of resources, which the project manager will need to manage?

   A. Quality management plan

   B. Resource management plan

   C. RACI chart

   D. Scope baseline

   ☑ **D.** The task Plan Resource Management takes only two inputs: the quality management plan and the scope baseline. The scope baseline identifies the deliverables from which you derive the type and quantity of resources required to create the deliverables.

   ⊠ **A**, **B**, and **C** are incorrect. **A** is incorrect because although it is one of the two inputs to the Plan Resource Management process, it is the scope baseline input that identifies the deliverables that drive which resources will be needed on the project. **B** is incorrect because the resource management plan is an output from the Plan Resource Management process. **C** is incorrect because RACI details roles and responsibilities of project stakeholders but does not identify resources needed.

10. Which process creates the resource breakdown structure?

   A. Acquire Resources

   B. Control Resources

   C. Estimate Activity Resources

   D. Plan Resource Management

   ☑ **C.** The Estimate Activity Resources process has the resource breakdown structure as an output.

   ⊠ **A**, **B**, and **D** are incorrect. Only the Estimate Activity Resources process has the resource breakdown structure as an output.

11. Which of the following is beneficial during the Planning phase in order to include relevant expertise and strengthen commitment to the project?

   A. The RACI chart

   B. Hiring an external consultant

   C. Identifying key performance indicators for requirements

   D. Participation of team members

   ☑ **D.** Although specific roles and responsibilities for project team members may exist, involving the entire team in project planning and decision making gives them a chance to add their expertise and results in strengthening their commitment to the project.

☒ **A**, **B**, and **C** are incorrect. **A** is incorrect because although specific roles and responsibilities for project team members may exist and participating in planning may not be a specific role and responsibility, involving the team shares ownership for the result. **B** is incorrect because hiring an external consultant may bring in expertise but will also usually result in the team members needing to be coached into high-performance mode. **C** is incorrect because identifying key performance indicators for the requirements portion of the project is specific to the Collect Requirements process and will not strengthen the commitment of all team members, just the business analysts.

12. As leader and manager of the project team, which of the following should the project manager be aware of as external project factors that may influence the project team?

   A. Names of the project sponsor and business analyst

   B. Quantitative and qualitative project risks

   C. Internal and external politics

   D. Business requirements and functional requirements

   ☑ **C.** Internal and external politics are factors outside the team that can influence team performance.

   ☒ **A**, **B**, and **D** are incorrect. Each of these represents aspects that are internal to the project; the question asks about factors external to the project.

13. As the project manager, if you place an order for low-quality material in order to stay within the project budget, what is the exposure to the project or project team?

   A. There is risk that quality of the product may be compromised causing rework.

   B. There is a risk that deadlines may not be met.

   C. There is a risk that the project team will require training.

   D. There is a risk that the project sponsor will initiate a change request.

   ☑ **A.** A choice in ordering low-quality materials can result in the risk that the materials could fail or cause rework. This is an example of failing to manage and control resources efficiently.

   ☒ **B**, **C**, and **D** are incorrect. Although each is a project risk, none are directly related to the choice to order low-quality materials.

14. What are teams called that function with an absence of centralized control?

   A. Specialists

   B. Subject matter experts

   C. Self-organizing

   D. Self-sufficient

   ☑ **C.** Agile approaches have made self-organizing teams popular, with a central tenet of these teams being that they rely on one another and function without a central authority or control.

⊠ **A**, **B**, and **D** are incorrect. **A** is incorrect because a self-organizing team can consist of generalized specialists, but a specialist by itself is not representing the entire team. **B** is incorrect because subject matter experts are more typical in predictive (nonadaptive) projects. **D** is incorrect because self-sufficient is actually not sufficient; a good team makes use of all available resources, including those where talent is needed from outside the team.

15. In a matrix management situation, which process is used to prevent unauthorized or conflicting assignments for team members between tasks for the functional manager and tasks for the project team?

    A. Monitor and Control Project Work

    B. Perform Integrated Change Control

    C. Control Resources

    D. Control Human Resources

    ☑ **C.** Ensuring that the assigned resources are available to the project at the right time and in the right place is a key goal of the Control Resources process.

    ⊠ **A**, **B**, and **D** are incorrect. **A** is incorrect because the Monitor and Control Project Work process is concerned with comparing actual project performance against the project management plan. **B** is incorrect because the process of coordinating changes across the entire project, including changes to cost, quality, schedule, and scope, is the Perform Integrated Change Control process. **D** is incorrect because there is no task involving human resources (HR) in the PMBOK; HR is typically a functional area within an organization.

16. Your company is undergoing a 12 percent reduction in workforce, and the project you are managing is affected. What should you do next?

    A. Carefully monitor and control the scarce resources.

    B. Request a preassigned contractor for needed resources.

    C. Suggest that a contracting officer representative (COR) be used for all project procurements.

    D. Use MoSCoW to reprioritize the work in your project.

    ☑ **A.** Projects need resources, and in this question resources are scarce. The task therefore lies with the project manager to determine the proper timing of those resources within the project schedule.

    ⊠ **B**, **C**, and **D** are incorrect. **B** is incorrect because preassignment allows you to select team members in advance, before the project starts. Team members may be assigned in the Develop Project Charter process. **C** is incorrect because not every project has a COR. **D** is incorrect because the MoSCoW method is not the only technique for prioritizing work in a project. MoSCoW = Must have, Should have, Could have, and Won't have.

17. Which estimation technique performs the estimation at the activity level and then aggregates up to develop estimates for work packages, control accounts, and summary project levels?

    A. Expert judgment

    B. Bottom-up estimating

    C. Analogous estimating

    D. Parametric estimating

    ☑ **B.** Bottom-up estimation is done by taking estimates from team and physical resources at the activity level and then summing and averaging them to develop estimates for work packages as well as control accounts and summary project information.

    ☒ **A, C,** and **D** are incorrect. **A** is incorrect because expert judgment information is used together with estimates from experts but not directly for work packages. **C** is incorrect because analogous estimating uses a similar project to form estimates for the current project. **D** is incorrect because parametric estimation involves using a parameter value as part of a calculation for an estimate.

18. Which process monitors and measures resources to ensure committed resources are made available and allocated according to the project management plan?

    A. Control Staffing

    B. Control Team

    C. Control Scope

    D. Control Resources

    ☑ **D.** Control Resources is the process of measuring and monitoring all project resources, and their associated costs, according to the project management plan. It is the process of managing resources to ensure the committed resources are made available to the project consistent with the commitments, resources are allocated within the project according to the plan, and resources are released from the project as dictated by the plan.

    ☒ **A, B,** and **C** are incorrect. **A** and **B** are incorrect because Control Staffing and Control Team are not phrases used in the *PMBOK Guide*. **C** is incorrect because Control Scope monitors project and product status and maps changes to the scope baseline.

19. Your current project is in trouble per reports from the company's project steering committee, with many of the project issues stemming from a lack of resources. What should you do immediately?

    A. Tell the steering committee you have analyzed the work performance data, and the work performance reports are wrong.

    B. Start with general and background information about the project's performance.

C. The problems from lack of resources have been noted in variance and trend analysis reports, which you are bringing to the project steering committee to justify more resources.

D. You now need to re-baseline the project's schedule because of the resource shortage.

☑ **B.** Presenting a chart of the project's performance over time will show how the performance is deteriorating because of scarce resources.

☒ **A, C,** and **D** are incorrect. **A** is incorrect because work performance data is the raw measurement of start and finish dates of schedule activities. Work performance information, such as the status of deliverables, is represented in work performance reports. You may use the documents to raise awareness of the resource problem after you show the impact over time of the resource problem. **C** is incorrect because the responsibilities of a project steering committee (PSC) in a project management setting include project priority setting and resource allocation, which are usually done after the PSC understands the resource allocation situation. **D** is incorrect because you have re-baselined the project's schedule and identified the corrective or preventive action required each time a due date is missed.

20. Which problem-solving technique focuses on achieving a win-win situation?

   A. Compromise/reconcile

   B. Collaborate/problem solve

   C. Force/direct

   D. Smooth/accommodate

☑ **B.** The conflict resolution technique of collaborating and problem solving, which incorporates multiple viewpoints and insights from differing perspectives, requires a cooperative attitude and open dialogue. The goal is to obtain consensus and commitment that results in a win-win situation.

☒ **A, C,** and **D** are incorrect. Collaboration/problem solving leads to a win-win situation by incorporating differing viewpoints and insights more so than compromise or reconciliation, forcing or directing, or smoothing or accommodating.

21. Which data representation shows the company's existing departments, units, or teams together with project activities as work packages listed under each department?

   A. Hierarchical charts

   B. Work breakdown structure

   C. Organizational breakdown structure

   D. Resource breakdown structure

☑ **C.** The organizational breakdown structure (OBS) shows organizational units such as departments, units, or teams and the project activities for each organizational unit.

☒ **A**, **B**, and **D** are incorrect. **A** is incorrect because an organizational breakdown structure is an example of the category of hierarchical charts so the more specific answer of organizational breakdown structure is the better answer. **B** is incorrect because a work breakdown structure shows how project deliverables decompose into work packages. **D** is incorrect because the resource breakdown structure is a hierarchical team list that also includes physical resources with categories and resource types.

22. Which Project Resource Management group process uses multiple data representations as a technique for carrying out the process?

   A. Acquire Resources

   B. Control Resources

   C. Estimate Activity Resources

   D. Plan Resource Management

   ☑ **D.** Only the Plan Resource Management process in the Project Resource Management process group includes data representations as a tool and technique. Histogram charts such as the WBS, OBS, and RBS are indicated for this process.

   ☒ **A**, **B**, and **C** are incorrect. Only the Plan Resource Management process in Project Resource Management includes data representations as a tool and technique.

23. Given that multiple methods are available to document team member roles as a part of the Project Resource Management process, what are the shared objectives of all of the methods?

   A. Ensure each work package has an ambiguous owner.

   B. Ensure team members have a clear understanding of their roles and responsibilities.

   C. Create an organizational breakdown structure.

   D. Create a resource breakdown structure.

   ☑ **B.** All data representations in Project Resource Management have two goals: ensure each work package has an unambiguous owner, and ensure team members have a clear understanding of their roles and responsibilities.

   ☒ **A**, **C**, and **D** are incorrect. **A** is incorrect because each work package should have an unambiguous owner. **C** and **D** are incorrect for the same reason: each of these is a data representation technique, and neither by itself states the goal for all data representations.

24. Which of the following will lead to the project manager tailoring the approach to Project Resource Management?

   A. Knowing whether the requirements will be captured with a formal or informal framework

   B. Identifying the risk threshold of the project sponsor

C. Identifying the risk threshold of the project customer

D. Knowing whether the team resources will be full-time or part-time

☑ **D.** Knowing whether the team resources will be full-time or part-time will help the project manager decide how to acquire resources for the project.

☒ **A, B**, and **C** are incorrect. **A** is incorrect because formal or informal approaches to requirements will tailor the approach to the Collect Requirements process but will not directly influence the Project Resource Management processes. **B** and **C** are incorrect because risk thresholds are important but will not directly influence the Project Resource Management processes.

Project Communications Management

In this chapter, you will

- Understand the three project management processes in the Project Communications Management knowledge area
- Identify the inputs, tools, techniques and outputs defined in the three Project Communications Management processes
- Identify key concepts and approaches in Project Communications Management, including tailoring and special considerations for agile/adaptive environments
- Recognize the dimensions of communication and components of a communications management plan
- Identify communications skills and methods for Project Communications Management

The Project Communications Management knowledge area accounts for 10 percent (30) of the questions on the CAPM exam. The *PMBOK Guide, Sixth Edition*, Sections 10.1 through 10.3, cover the three processes in the Project Communications Management knowledge area.

This chapter focuses on Project Communications Management. Like the other knowledge areas, it begins with a process of planning, which produces a communications management plan. It then has an executing process, Manage Communications, focusing on carrying out the communications management plan, and a monitoring and controlling process, Monitor Communications, focused on checking whether project communications are meeting stakeholder communication requirements.

Project Communications Management is focused upon the processes of developing a communications management plan, gathering and distributing project information according to that plan, and checking that you are completing the communications activities in accordance with the plan.

Project communications are critical for a smooth and successful running of any project, whether you are gathering information or disseminating information. You should assume that a project manager will, in fact, spend 90 percent of his or her time communicating in different ways, different forms, and to different stakeholders. Of this time spent communicating, 50 percent will be spent communicating with project team members because they are the most important of the stakeholders.

The 30 practice questions in this chapter are mapped to the style and frequency of question types you will see on the CAPM exam.

1. Which of the following processes produces the communications management plan?

   A. Develop Project Management Plan

   B. Plan Communications Management

   C. Manage Communications

   D. Develop Communications Management Plan

2. The decision to use a written document to provide project updates is an example of what type of tool or technique?

   A. Communication technology

   B. Communication models

   C. Expert judgment

   D. Meetings

3. What is the name of the tool that analyzes the individual communication requirements for each of the stakeholders?

   A. Communication models

   B. Information management systems

   C. Communications requirements analysis

   D. Communications technology

4. When you send a handwritten update to project stakeholders and they are unable to read your handwriting, what is this an example of?

   A. Bad handwriting

   B. Noise

   C. Interference

   D. Feedback

5. You have set up an intranet site for project team members to be able to download project progress updates. This is an example of which method of communication?

   A. Interactive

   B. Push

   C. Pull

   D. Manual

6. How does the project kick-off meeting act as a means of communication?

   A. The kick-off meeting does not act as a means of communication.

   B. The kick-off meeting signals to the team that enough planning has been completed to begin execution.

C. The kick-off meeting is completed to start project initiation, and therefore it informs the team that the project is about to start.

D. The kick-off meeting signals the beginning of project closure and communicates to the team that the job is done.

7. What is the correct sequence of the following terms?

A. Work performance report, work performance data, work performance information

B. Work performance information, work performance data, work performance report

C. Work performance data, work performance report, work performance information

D. Work performance data, work performance information, work performance report

8. If you are engaged in consciously paying attention to body language and trying to understand the communication from a sender, what are you involved in?

A. Active listening

B. Effective listening

C. Providing feedback

D. Paralingual communication

9. All the following are examples of communication skills except:

A. Reviewing the work breakdown structure to ensure team members know what has to be done

B. Setting and managing expectations

C. Persuading a person or organization to perform an action

D. Listening actively and effectively

10. What sort of communication is most appropriate when dealing with changes to a contract?

A. Informal written

B. Formal written

C. Formal verbal

D. Electronic

11. All the following are factors that influence the method of communication disbursement between team members except:

A. Availability of technology

B. Duration of the project

C. Local government regulations

D. Urgency of the need for information

12. All the following communications are noise except:

    A. Educational differences

    B. Differences in motivation

    C. Lack of a communications device

    D. Cultural differences

13. What technique could help you to understand better when you are having difficulty concentrating on what a stakeholder is saying during a business meeting and you feel you are not fully understanding them?

    A. Repeat the message back to the stakeholder.

    B. Ask them to write everything down.

    C. Ask to postpone the meeting until you feel better.

    D. Ask them to speak slower.

14. When you ask that all correspondence be conducted in English, what are you trying to minimize in your team's communications?

    A. Environmental constraints

    B. Cultural differences

    C. Noise

    D. Foreign accents

15. Which of the following is a characteristic of a good listener?

    A. Takes good notes

    B. Repeats some of the things said

    C. Finishes the speaker's sentences

    D. Agrees with the speaker

16. What sort of communication method is being used when sending out your weekly project update to a wide range of stakeholders?

    A. Stakeholder management strategy

    B. Pull communication

    C. Interactive communication

    D. Push communication

17. What sort of communication method are you using when you use the intranet site to post large amounts of information that team members can log in to read?

    A. Encoding and decoding

    B. Push communication

    C. Interactive communication

    D. Pull communication

18. Who should take responsibility when the team is disagreeing about what, how, and when different communication methods are to be used?

    A. Stakeholder representative

    B. Project team

    C. Project sponsor

    D. Project manager

19. Which of the following would you not expect to find in your communications management plan?

    A. Person responsible for authorizing the release of confidential information

    B. Team members' addresses and phone numbers

    C. Glossary of common terminology

    D. Stakeholder communication requirements

20. All the following are techniques to ensure your project meetings are more productive except?

    A. Teleconferencing

    B. Ground rules

    C. A start and finish time for the meeting

    D. An agenda

21. Effective information distribution includes all of the following techniques except:

    A. Writing style

    B. Presentation techniques

    C. Issue log

    D. Choice of media

22. The Manage Communications process occurs within which *PMBOK Guide* process group?

    A. Initiating

    B. Planning

    C. Executing

    D. Monitoring and controlling

23. How important is nonverbal communication to negotiations?

    A. Very important

    B. Not very important

    C. Only important when the other party is silent

    D. Only important during negotiations over cost

24. What is the best form of communication to use when dealing with unacceptable behavior towards other project team members?

 A. Formal written

 B. Formal verbal

 C. Informal written

 D. Informal verbal

25. What information and method would be best to use when presenting a detailed project update to some high-level stakeholders?

 A. A verbal presentation during a 10-minute meeting

 B. A summary milestone report tabled as an agenda item at their next scheduled meeting

 C. A PowerPoint presentation outlining the major issues given in your office

 D. A detailed performance report in writing with an accompanying presentation and time for questions and answers

26. What is the best term to describe when cultural differences and using unfamiliar technology are the main communication problems?

 A. Decoding

 B. Feedback

 C. Noise

 D. Transmission

27. Which of the following would be least useful to you when you are actively monitoring and controlling the project communications according to your approved communications management plan?

 A. Project communications

 B. Issue log

 C. Work performance data

 D. Change requests

28. Which of the following forecasting methods is an example of using historical data about your project to forecast an estimated future outcome in your project performance reporting?

 A. Budget forecasts

 B. Judgmental methods

 C. Econometric method

 D. Time series methods

29. What forecasting method are you using when you are currently assessing the information supplied anonymously by the respondents and plan to request a second round of opinions to use in your project forecasts?

    A. Judgmental method

    B. Causal method

    C. Earned value

    D. Econometric method

30. Which of the following would you not expect to see in a detailed project performance report?

    A. Current status of risks and issues

    B. Staff performance reviews

    C. Forecasted project completion

    D. Summary of changes approved in the period

1. B	11. C	21. C
2. A	12. C	22. C
3. C	13. A	23. A
4. B	14. C	24. A
5. C	15. B	25. D
6. B	16. D	26. C
7. D	17. D	27. D
8. B	18. D	28. D
9. A	19. B	29. A
10. B	20. A	30. B

1. Which of the following processes produces the communications management plan?

   A. Develop Project Management Plan

   B. Plan Communications Management

   C. Manage Communications

   D. Develop Communications Management Plan

   ☑ **B.** The main output from the Plan Communications Management process is the communications management plan.

   ☒ **A**, **C**, and **D** are incorrect. **A** is incorrect because the Develop Project Management Plan process produces the project management plan. **C** is incorrect because the Manage Communications process uses the communications management plan to gather, store, and distribute project information and communications. **D** is incorrect because Develop Communications Management Plan is a made-up process name.

2. The decision to use a written document to provide project updates is an example of what type of tool or technique?

   A. Communication technology

   B. Communication models

   C. Expert judgment

   D. Meetings

   ☑ **A.** Any decision you make about the technology used, whether manual or electronic, for the dissemination of project information is a decision about communication technology.

   ☒ **B**, **C**, and **D** are incorrect. **B** is incorrect because communication models explain what might happen between sender and receiver. **C** is incorrect because expert judgment is a tool used to assist with monitoring how well communications are going. **D** is incorrect because meetings are a tool used to help the project team understand and contribute to effective project communications.

3. What is the name of the tool that analyzes the individual communication requirements for each of the stakeholders?

   A. Communication models

   B. Information management systems

   C. Communications requirements analysis

   D. Communications technology

   ☑ **C.** Communications requirements analysis is the technique used to determine individual stakeholder communication requirements.

☒ **A**, **B**, and **D** are incorrect. **A** is incorrect because communications models explain what may happen to communications between sender and receiver. **B** is incorrect because information management systems are used to gather and store project information. **D** is incorrect because communications technology is a technique used to determine what form the communication will take.

4. When you send a handwritten update to project stakeholders and they are unable to read your handwriting, what is this an example of?

   A. Bad handwriting

   B. Noise

   C. Interference

   D. Feedback

   ☑ **B.** Any element that can interfere with the message is noise.

   ☒ **A**, **C**, and **D** are incorrect. **A** is incorrect because in the strictest sense of the word, it is an example of bad handwriting, but according to the basic communications model, it is an example of interference with the message, which is the definition of noise. **C** is incorrect because noise creates interference. **D** is incorrect because feedback is used by the receiver to send confirmation of the message received back to the sender.

5. You have set up an intranet site for project team members to be able to download project progress updates. This is an example of which method of communication?

   A. Interactive

   B. Push

   C. Pull

   D. Manual

   ☑ **C.** This is an example of pull communication, because the receivers download the information at their discretion.

   ☒ **A**, **B**, and **D** are incorrect. **A** is incorrect because interactive communication is where more than one person is involved in the communication at the same time. **B** is incorrect because push communication involves the sender sending the communication to the receiver. **D** is incorrect because manual communication refers to forms of communication that are not conducted electronically.

6. How does the project kick-off meeting act as a means of communication?

   A. The kick-off meeting does not act as a means of communication.

   B. The kick-off meeting signals to the team that enough planning has been completed to begin execution.

   C. The kick-off meeting is completed to start project initiation, and therefore it informs the team that the project is about to start.

   D. The kick-off meeting signals the beginning of project closure and communicates to the team that the job is done.

☑ **B.** The use of the kick-off meeting as both a functional meeting to discuss execution and as a team morale-building exercise means that it is an effective form of communication.

☒ **A, C,** and **D** are incorrect. **A** is incorrect because the kick-off meeting does act as a means of communication by communicating to the team that enough planning has been done to begin execution. **C** is incorrect because the kick-off meeting is completed after enough planning has been done to begin project execution and not at the beginning of project initiation. **D** is incorrect because the kick-off meeting does not begin the process of project closure.

7. What is the correct sequence of the following terms?

   A. Work performance report, work performance data, work performance information

   B. Work performance information, work performance data, work performance report

   C. Work performance data, work performance report, work performance information

   D. Work performance data, work performance information, work performance report

   ☑ **D.** This is the correct order: work performance data, which is the raw data gathered about project performance, which in turn gets filtered and refined as understandable work performance information, which in turn is selected to be included in work performance reports.

   ☒ **A, B,** and **C** are incorrect. **A** is incorrect because work performance reports come after work performance data and work performance information. **B** is incorrect because work performance data comes before work performance information. **C** is incorrect because work performance information comes before work performance reports.

8. If you are engaged in consciously paying attention to body language and trying to understand the communication from a sender, what are you involved in?

   A. Active listening

   B. Effective listening

   C. Providing feedback

   D. Paralingual communication

   ☑ **B.** Effective listening takes active listening one step further and has the receiver monitoring nonverbal cues such as body language.

   ☒ **A, C,** and **D** are incorrect. **A** is incorrect because active listening means that the receiver is actively engaged in trying to understand the message from the sender and does not necessarily involve paying attention to things like body language. **C** is incorrect because feedback doesn't necessarily involve the interpretation of body language. **D** is incorrect because paralingual communication involves recognizing and observing vocal but nonverbal communication clues such as expressions, inflections, tone, and volume of voice.

9. All the following are examples of communication skills except:

   A. Reviewing the work breakdown structure to ensure team members know what has to be done

   B. Setting and managing expectations

   C. Persuading a person or organization to perform an action

   D. Listening actively and effectively

   ☑ **A.** Reviewing the work breakdown structure is a technical, not a communication, skill. We cannot stress enough the role that effective communication plays in project success. Many people seem to think it is the technical, financial, risk, quality, and scope management skills that are more important contributors to project success. But without effective communication, they are all useless.

   ☒ **B, C,** and **D** are incorrect. **B** is incorrect because setting and managing the expectations of stakeholders is achieved through the effective use of communication skills. **C** is incorrect because to persuade a person or organization to perform an action, you will need to display very strong and well-developed communication skills. **D** is incorrect because communication is a two-way process, and therefore listening actively and effectively is a key communication skill.

10. What sort of communication is most appropriate when dealing with changes to a contract?

    A. Informal written

    B. Formal written

    C. Formal verbal

    D. Electronic

    ☑ **B.** A contract is a legally binding document, and as such all communication about contracts should be formal and in writing.

    ☒ **A, C,** and **D** are incorrect. **A** is incorrect because informal written forms of communication are best used for memos and internal notes. **C** is incorrect because formal verbal forms of communication are presentations and speeches. **D** is incorrect because electronic forms of communication include e-mails and the Internet. When dealing with changes to a contract, formal written forms of communication are best.

11. All the following are factors that influence the method of communication disbursement between team members except:

    A. Availability of technology

    B. Duration of the project

    C. Local government regulations

    D. Urgency of the need for information

    ☑ **C.** Local government regulations are related to building and town planning matters and may affect your project in other ways but will not affect the communication distribution method.

☒ **A**, **B**, and **D** are incorrect. **A** is incorrect because the type and availability of technology will influence the method of communications on your project. **B** is incorrect because the duration of the project will affect what style of communication you choose, as you will have to keep stakeholders effectively engaged over longer periods of time. **D** is incorrect because the urgency of the information will influence the choice of communication method. You must always select an appropriate method of communication to ensure it is effective.

12. All the following communications are noise except:
    A. Educational differences
    B. Differences in motivation
    C. Lack of a communications device
    D. Cultural differences

    ☑ **C.** Communication involves at least two people, who may have very different backgrounds, experience, and education. Many times these individuals come from different cultures, speak different languages, and certainly have different drivers.

    ☒ **A**, **B**, and **D** are incorrect. **A** is incorrect because education differences can present problems in communication, particularly in the languages and medium chosen to communicate. **B** is incorrect because if one party is motivated to be part of the conversation occurring and one isn't, then there will be a disruption to the communication. **D** is incorrect because cultural differences represent noise, because many misunderstandings can arise because of different cultural expectations around appropriate forms of communication.

13. What technique could help you to understand better when you are having difficulty concentrating on what a stakeholder is saying during a business meeting and you feel you are not fully understanding them?
    A. Repeat the message back to the stakeholder.
    B. Ask them to write everything down.
    C. Ask to postpone the meeting until you feel better.
    D. Ask them to speak slower.

    ☑ **A.** Part of effective communication is ensuring that the message from sender to receiver is decoded properly. An effective way to do this is to repeat the key points back to get clarity.

    ☒ **B**, **C**, and **D** are incorrect. **B** is incorrect because asking somebody to write down the message won't improve your ability to understand. The solution to this problem is actively engaging in effective listening. **C** is incorrect because it is your responsibility to ensure that you are actively engaged in effectively listening to a conversation, and postponing the meeting will only complicate communication matters. **D** is incorrect because the problem is not the speed at which the person is speaking—the problem is your ability to concentrate. To help you concentrate, you could simply repeat the message back to the stakeholder.

14. When you ask that all correspondence be conducted in English, what are you trying to minimize in your team's communications?

    A. Environmental constraints

    B. Cultural differences

    C. Noise

    D. Foreign accents

    ☑ **C.** Noise is the term used to describe anything that gets in the way of the message between sender and receiver. Using English as a common language is an attempt to avoid the noise of different languages.

    ☒ **A**, **B**, and **D** are incorrect. **A** is incorrect because by asking your project team to use English as a standardized language, you are not trying to minimize environmental constraints; you are trying to minimize noise and communications. **B** is incorrect because you are trying to minimize noise that may corrupt communications, not minimize cultural differences. **D** is incorrect because simply asking your team to use English as a standardized language does not minimize the use of foreign accents.

15. Which of the following is a characteristic of a good listener?

    A. Takes good notes

    B. Repeats some of the things said

    C. Finishes the speaker's sentences

    D. Agrees with the speaker

    ☑ **B.** Good listening is an important skill for any manager. One of the ways that you can become a skilled listener is by repeating some of the things that are said. Summarizing gives yourself and others a repetition of important points and makes the speaker feel more relaxed and in a friendly atmosphere.

    ☒ **A**, **C**, and **D** are incorrect. **A** is incorrect because taking good notes is an example of a good note taker, not a good listener. **C** is incorrect because finishing the speaker's sentences is often considered quite rude and not the sign of a good listener. **D** is incorrect because simply agreeing with the speaker without a good reason is not a sign of a good listener.

16. What sort of communication method is being used when sending out your weekly project update to a wide range of stakeholders?

    A. Stakeholder management strategy

    B. Pull communication

    C. Interactive communication

    D. Push communication

   ☑ **D.** In this instance you are pushing the information out to stakeholders. Push communication occurs when the sender pushes the information to the recipient.

   ☒ **A, B,** and **C** are incorrect. **A** is incorrect because the stakeholder management strategy may guide some of your communications, particularly those in relation to stakeholder expectation management, but it is not a type of communication method. **B** is incorrect because pull communication occurs when the recipient must go to the source to get the communication. **C** is incorrect because interactive communication occurs when both sender and recipient engage in a mutual exchange of information.

17. What sort of communication method are you using when you use the intranet site to post large amounts of information that team members can log in to read?

   A. Encoding and decoding

   B. Push communication

   C. Interactive communication

   D. Pull communication

   ☑ **D.** It is called pull communication because recipients pull it down at their convenience, rather than having it pushed to them.

   ☒ **A, B,** and **C** are incorrect. **A** is incorrect because encoding and decoding are what senders and receivers do in the standard communications model. **B** is incorrect because push communication occurs when the sender pushes the information to the recipient. **C** is incorrect because interactive communication occurs when both sender and recipient engage in a mutual exchange of information.

18. Who should take responsibility when the team is disagreeing about what, how, and when different communication methods are to be used?

   A. Stakeholder representative

   B. Project team

   C. Project sponsor

   D. Project manager

   ☑ **D.** It is the responsibility of the project manager to decide what, how, and when communication methods are to be used in the project.

   ☒ **A, B,** and **C** are incorrect. **A** is incorrect because the responsibility does not lie with any representative of a stakeholder, which could refer to anybody at all. The responsibility lies with the project manager. **B** is incorrect because the project team should not be left to make this decision; it is the responsibility of the project manager. **C** is incorrect because this issue does not need to be escalated to the project sponsor, as it is the responsibility of the project manager to make this decision.

19. Which of the following would you not expect to find in your communications management plan?

    A. Person responsible for authorizing the release of confidential information

    B. Team members' addresses and phone numbers

    C. Glossary of common terminology

    D. Stakeholder communication requirements

    ☑ **B.** You would not normally find information as specific as team member addresses and phone numbers in the communications management plan.

    ☒ **A**, **C**, and **D** are incorrect. **A** is incorrect because the communications management plan will refer to the person who has responsibility for authorizing release of confidential information to stakeholders. **C** is incorrect because for ease of use and standardization, it is typical for the communications management plan to have a glossary of common terminology. **D** is incorrect because at the core of the communication management plan will be stakeholder communication requirements.

20. All the following are techniques to ensure your project meetings are more productive except?

    A. Teleconferencing

    B. Ground rules

    C. A start and finish time for the meeting

    D. An agenda

    ☑ **A.** Meetings need to have structure around them, and setting an agenda, ground rules, and a set time for the meeting to run are good ways of improving efficiency. Teleconferencing is not a standardized way to make meetings more productive. Normally, the preference would be for participants to meet face to face.

    ☒ **B**, **C**, and **D** are incorrect. **B** is incorrect because establishing ground rules for attendance, conduct, and follow-up will make a meeting more productive. **C** is incorrect because setting clear start and finish times for the meeting so participants know when they should be there and when they will return to work is a way to make meetings more productive. **D** is incorrect because a clear and defined agenda that is followed will make meetings more efficient and productive.

21. Effective information distribution includes all of the following techniques except:

    A. Writing style

    B. Presentation techniques

    C. Issue log

    D. Choice of media

☑ **C.** The issue log can be used as a communications tool to let stakeholders know these are being monitored, but it is not a means of information distribution itself.

☒ **A**, **B**, and **D** are incorrect. **A** is incorrect because selecting the appropriate writing style to match the stakeholder needs is an effective information distribution technique. **B** is incorrect because presentation techniques are a very effective way of distributing information to stakeholders. **D** is incorrect because selecting the correct and appropriate choice of media is an effective information distribution technique.

22. The Manage Communications process occurs within which *PMBOK Guide* process group?

   A. Initiating

   B. Planning

   C. Executing

   D. Monitoring and controlling

   ☑ **C.** Manage Communications is part of the Executing process group.

   ☒ **A**, **B**, and **D** are incorrect. Manage Communications is part of the Executing process group.

23. How important is nonverbal communication to negotiations?

   A. Very important

   B. Not very important

   C. Only important when the other party is silent

   D. Only important during negotiations over cost

   ☑ **A.** Humans are complex communicators, and the nonverbal communications we use are always very important and can, at times, be more important than the verbal communications.

   ☒ **B**, **C**, and **D** are incorrect. Humans are complex communicators, and the nonverbal communications we use are always very important and can, at times, be more important than the verbal communications.

24. What is the best form of communication to use when dealing with unacceptable behavior towards other project team members?

   A. Formal written

   B. Formal verbal

   C. Informal written

   D. Informal verbal

   ☑ **A.** Because this situation is a serious one that needs to be documented for future reference, it would be best to use formal written forms of communication.

☒ **B**, **C**, and **D** are incorrect. **B** is incorrect because using formal verbal, or any verbal, form of communication could mean that the message was understood but forgotten. So in this instance, a formal written form of communication is best. **C** is incorrect because this situation is a serious one and needs to be documented for future reference. It would be best to use formal, rather than informal, written forms of communication. **D** is incorrect because using informal verbal, or any verbal, form of communication could mean that the message was understood and forgotten. So in this instance a formal written form of communication is best.

25. What information and method would be best to use when presenting a detailed project update to some high-level stakeholders?

   A. A verbal presentation during a 10-minute meeting

   B. A summary milestone report tabled as an agenda item at their next scheduled meeting

   C. A PowerPoint presentation outlining the major issues given in your office

   D. A detailed performance report in writing with an accompanying presentation and time for questions and answers

   ☑ **D.** Choosing the most appropriate information and the way in which you deliver it is an important decision to ensure the efficacy of your project reporting.

   ☒ **A**, **B**, and **C** are incorrect. **A** is incorrect because a verbal presentation given casually during a 10-minute meeting will not contain the detailed information the stakeholders are looking for. **B** is incorrect because a summary milestone report will not contain the detailed information that stakeholders are looking for. **C** is incorrect because a PowerPoint presentation outlining the major issues will not contain the detailed information the stakeholders are looking for.

26. What is the best term to describe when cultural differences and using unfamiliar technology are the main communication problems?

   A. Decoding

   B. Feedback

   C. Noise

   D. Transmission

   ☑ **C.** In the standard communications model, noise refers to any obstacle in the selected medium between sender and receiver that can affect the communication.

   ☒ **A**, **B**, and **D** are incorrect. **A** is incorrect because decoding is the process that the receiver of the message does once the message has been received. **B** is incorrect because feedback is a process where the receiver provides feedback to the sender of the message to facilitate more effective listening. **D** is incorrect because transmission is the process of communicating a message via a selected medium.

27. Which of the following would be least useful to you when you are actively monitoring and controlling the project communications according to your approved communications management plan?

A. Project communications

B. Issue log

C. Work performance data

D. Change requests

☑ **D.** The question is asking about the inputs into the Control Communications process, and change requests are an output from, not an input in, this process.

☒ **A**, **B**, and **C** are incorrect. **A** is incorrect because the project communications are an input into the Control Communications process. **B** is incorrect because the issue log is an input into the Control Communications process. **C** is incorrect because work performance data is an input into the Control Communications process.

28. Which of the following forecasting methods is an example of using historical data about your project to forecast an estimated future outcome in your project performance reporting?

A. Budget forecasts

B. Judgmental methods

C. Econometric method

D. Time series methods

☑ **D.** This is an example of a time series method, such as earned value.

☒ **A**, **B**, and **C** are incorrect. **A** is incorrect because budget forecasts are part of earned value management, which is an example of a time series method. Time series is the best answer. **B** is incorrect because the judgmental forecasting method uses methods from experts, such as the Delphi method. **C** is incorrect because econometric methods use tools such as linear regression.

29. What forecasting method are you using when you are currently assessing the information supplied anonymously by the respondents and plan to request a second round of opinions to use in your project forecasts?

A. Judgmental method

B. Causal method

C. Earned value

D. Econometric method

☑ **A.** This is an example of using the Delphi technique, which is an example of a judgmental forecasting method.

☒ **B**, **C**, and **D** are incorrect. **B** is incorrect because causal is another name for econometric methods, which use tools such as linear regression. **C** is incorrect because earned value is one example of a time series method. **D** is incorrect because econometric methods use tools such as linear regression.

30. Which of the following would you not expect to see in a detailed project performance report?

    A. Current status of risks and issues

    B. Staff performance reviews

    C. Forecasted project completion

    D. Summary of changes approved in the period

    ☑ **B.** Staff performance review information is not generally included in project performance reports. They would be included in team assessments.

    ☒ **A, C,** and **D** are incorrect. **A** is incorrect because the current status of risks and issues is a crucial component of a detailed project performance report. **C** is incorrect because the forecasted project completion would definitely be included in a detailed project performance report to provide a project status update. **D** is incorrect because a clear summary of changes approved since the last report would definitely be included in a detailed project performance report to understand the scope change.

Project Risk Management

In this chapter, you will

- Understand the seven project management processes in the Project Risk Management knowledge area
- Identify the inputs, tools, techniques, and outputs defined in Project Risk Management
- Identify the key documents in Project Risk Management
- Perform simple risk calculations
- Recognize when and how to adjust risk based on the project environment

Managing risk is a central theme for a project manager, and indeed for the entire project team. Certified Associate in Project Management (CAPM) candidates are tested on five important risk objectives in order to demonstrate full knowledge of the impact of risks on a project. To pass the CAPM® exam, a candidate must know what risks are, how risks can affect a project, and the role that each project team member and project manager has in ensuring that risk does not derail a project.

The 24 practice questions in this chapter are mapped to the style and frequency of question types you will see on the CAPM exam.

1. What is the difference between verified deliverables and accepted deliverables?

    A. Accepted deliverables are inputs to Validate Scope, whereas verified deliverables are outputs from Validate Scope.

    B. Accepted deliverables are created by the Control Quality process, and verified deliverables are created in the Closing process group.

    C. Verified deliverables are inputs to the Control Quality process, whereas accepted deliverables are outputs from the Closing process group.

    D. Verified deliverables are inputs to Validate Scope, whereas accepted deliverables are outputs from Validate Scope.

2. How often should an organization address risk management during a project?

    A. At every management meeting

    B. Only in the planning phase

    C. On high-risk projects only

    D. Consistently throughout

3. The PMO guidelines for all projects at your company advise that a project should have a balance between risk taking and risk avoidance. This policy is implemented in a project using:

    A. Risk responses

    B. Risk analysis

    C. Risk identification

    D. Risk classification

4. Who is responsible for identifying risks in a new project?

    A. The project manager

    B. The project sponsor

    C. Any project personnel

    D. The main stakeholders

5. The document that contains a list of identified risks, a list of potential responses for each risk, the root cause of the risk, and the risk category is called the:

    A. Risk management plan

    B. Project issues log

    C. Risk category checklist

    D. Risk register

6. As part of your responsibility for managing risks in your project, you rate risks as low, medium, or high. What tool would you typically use to define these categories?

   A. Probability impact matrix

   B. Risk register updates

   C. Assumption analysis

   D. Checklist analysis

7. A new member of your project team suggests that you should quantify risks using the lowest, highest, and most likely costs of the WBS elements in the project plan. What is the name for the technique being suggested?

   A. Three-point estimating

   B. Probability impact analysis

   C. Probability distributions

   D. Sensitivity analysis

8. The process of project planning that involves developing options, determining actions to enhance opportunities, and reducing threats to project objectives is called (a):

   A. Perform Qualitative Risk Analysis

   B. Plan Risk Responses

   C. Perform Quantitative Risk Analysis

   D. Probability Impact Matrix

9. Your team is developing a part of the risk management plan. For some of the risks, the team decides that a response plan will be executed only when certain predefined conditions exist. What is the term given to this type of risk strategy?

   A. Contingent

   B. Sharing

   C. Exploit

   D. Enhance

10. Information such as outcomes of risk reassessments, risk audits, and periodic risk reviews are examples from which of the following?

    A. Risk management plan

    B. Approved change requests

    C. Project document updates

    D. Work performance information

11. As part of implementing risk responses, you are updating your risk report. You should include:

    A. Any changes to overall risk exposure

    B. Impact of identified risks on achieving project benefits

    C. A change request process for risks that occur that affect project team assignments

    D. A revised list of prioritized issues that affect the project's objectives

12. In the Implement Risk Responses process, which of the following is done for each risk?

    A. Specify the risk thresholds based on the risk appetite of the sponsor.

    B. Encourage risk owners to take necessary action, if required.

    C. Document the risk description and impact if it happens.

    D. Inform project stakeholders of all ranked risks.

13. What are you engaged in if you are documenting the effectiveness of risk responses in dealing with identified risks and their root causes, as well as the effectiveness of the risk management process?

    A. Implement risk responses

    B. Risk identification

    C. Risk analysis

    D. Risk audit

14. In which process does a project manager prioritize individual risks by assessing their probability of occurrence and impact?

    A. Plan Risk Management

    B. Identify Risks

    C. Perform Qualitative Risk Analysis

    D. Perform Quantitative Risk Analysis

15. In which process does the project manager numerically analyze the combined effect of identified individual project risks and other sources of uncertainty on overall project objectives?

    A. Plan Risk Management

    B. Identify Risks

    C. Perform Qualitative Risk Analysis

    D. Perform Quantitative Risk Analysis

16. Calculate EMV for a risk event that has a 40 percent chance of occurring and that, if it occurred, would cost the project an additional $100,000.

    A. $4,000

    B. $40,000

C. $100,000

D. $400,000

17. Risk A has a 50 percent chance of happening. Unrelated Risk B has a 20 percent chance of happening. What is the chance they will both happen?

A. 10 percent

B. 30 percent

C. 70 percent

D. 100 percent

18. If the EMV of a risk is $200,000 and this risk exposure has been documented in the project business case, what is the maximum you could spend to remove the risk completely and be better off?

A. $20,000

B. $100,000

C. $2,000,000

D. $200,000

19. A residual risk is assessed to have a probability of 0.1 and an impact value of $50,000. What is the EMV of the residual risk?

A. $1,000

B. $5,000

C. $50,000

D. EMV does not apply to residual risk

20. How is secondary risk assessed?

A. $E = (a + 4m + b) / 6$

B. EMV plus 10 percent

C. Determine probability and multiply by impact

D. The same way as original or residual risks

21. In order to prepare the risk management plan, what should a project manager define first?

A. Your organization's risk appetite

B. The functional requirements document you plan to use to identify risks

C. The resisting stakeholders

D. Budget assumptions and constraints

22. You are preparing to lead a project team creating a product that is expected to be available for the Christmas buying season and is anticipated to be popular with young adults ages 25 to 35. What should you be sure to review before finalizing the risk management plan for this particular project?

A. Occupational safety and health issues

B. Business case

C. Potential suppliers on the prequalified sellers list

D. Cultural differences in the production workers

23. You have a design team of seven members and a support team of three people; these numbers are about half of what you believe you need. These limits are examples of:

A. Constraints to document in your project scope statement

B. Limitations to document in your project charter

C. Known risks to set aside management reserves

D. Key issues to document in the risk log

24. A generally accepted business practice to follow regarding risks and issues is to:

A. Use the risk register to capture operational-level issues

B. Set up a risk control board for risks and issues that may occur

C. Set up an escalation process for you to help resolve risks and issues

D. Ensure a risk or issue is isolated to a single project phase

1. D		**9.** A		**17.** A	
2. D		**10.** C		**18.** D	
3. A		**11.** A		**19.** B	
4. C		**12.** B		**20.** D	
5. D		**13.** D		**21.** A	
6. A		**14.** C		**22.** B	
7. A		**15.** D		**23.** A	
8. B		**16.** B		**24.** C	

1. What is the difference between verified deliverables and accepted deliverables?

    A. Accepted deliverables are inputs to Validate Scope, whereas verified deliverables are outputs from Validate Scope.

    B. Accepted deliverables are created by the Control Quality process, and verified deliverables are created in the Closing process group.

    C. Verified deliverables are inputs to the Control Quality process, whereas accepted deliverables are outputs from the Closing process group.

    D. Verified deliverables are inputs to Validate Scope, whereas accepted deliverables are outputs from Validate Scope.

    ☑ **D**. Verified deliverables are created in the Control Quality process and are inputs to Validate Scope, whereas accepted deliverables are outputs from the Validate Scope process.

    ☒ **A**, **B**, and **C** are incorrect. Verifying deliverables is an internal project activity performed in the Control Quality process, whereas accepting the deliverables requires that the customer (external from the team) formally accepts and signs off on verified deliverables from the project team, making them "accepted" deliverables.

2. How often should an organization address risk management during a project?

    A. At every management meeting

    B. Only in the planning phase

    C. On high-risk projects only

    D. Consistently throughout

    ☑ **D**. An organization should be committed to addressing risk management proactively and consistently throughout the project.

    ☒ **A**, **B**, and **C** are incorrect. Risk needs to be identified early, with mitigation strategies in place, and then constantly monitored as the details of the project are progressively elaborated to ensure that new risks have not been introduced.

3. The PMO guidelines for all projects at your company advise that a project should have a balance between risk taking and risk avoidance. This policy is implemented in a project using:

    A. Risk responses

    B. Risk analysis

    C. Risk identification

    D. Risk classification

    ☑ **A**. A balance between risk taking and risk avoidance is the application of risk responses.

    ☒ **B**, **C**, and **D** are incorrect. Risk analysis, risk identification, and risk classification are parts of prior steps to the responses in the Risk Management process.

4. Who is responsible for identifying risks in a new project?

   A. The project manager

   B. The project sponsor

   C. Any project personnel

   D. The main stakeholders

   ☑ C. Any project personnel can identify risks in a project.

   ☒ A, B, and D are incorrect. Any project personnel can identify risks. The project manager manages the Risk Management process, with input from the sponsor and main stakeholders.

5. The document that contains a list of identified risks, a list of potential responses for each risk, the root cause of the risk, and the risk category is called the:

   A. Risk management plan

   B. Project issues log

   C. Risk category checklist

   D. Risk register

   ☑ D. A list of identified risks, a list of potential responses for each risk, the root cause of the risk, and the risk category are the basic fields in a risk register.

   ☒ A, B, and C are incorrect. A is incorrect because the risk management plan is the overall management document and processes definitions for managing risk in the project. B is incorrect because the project issues log contains the list of all issues, not solely risks. C is incorrect because the risk category checklist contains weighting information on probability and impact.

6. As part of your responsibility for managing risks in your project, you rate risks as low, medium, or high. What tool would you typically use to define these categories?

   A. Probability impact matrix

   B. Risk register updates

   C. Assumption analysis

   D. Checklist analysis

   ☑ A. Rating risks into a low, medium, or high category is performed and presented on a probability impact matrix.

   ☒ B, C, and D are incorrect. B is incorrect because risk register updates are an output from the Risk Management process. C and D are incorrect because assumption analysis and checklist analysis are tools used for risk identification.

7. A new member of your project team suggests that you should quantify risks using the lowest, highest, and most likely costs of the WBS elements in the project plan. What is the name for the technique being suggested?

A. Three-point estimating

B. Probability impact analysis

C. Probability distributions

D. Sensitivity analysis

☑ **A.** Three-point estimating is a technique that is often used for risk analysis that calculates or obtains information on the lowest, highest, and most likely costs of the WBS elements in the project plan.

☒ **B, C,** and **D** are incorrect. **B** is incorrect because probability impact analysis is a ranking of risks. **C** is incorrect because probability distributions are the application of three-point estimates in different ways. **D** is incorrect because sensitivity analysis is used to test the major project variables independently for risks.

8. The process of project planning that involves developing options, determining actions to enhance opportunities, and reducing threats to project objectives is called (a):

A. Perform Qualitative Risk Analysis

B. Plan Risk Responses

C. Perform Quantitative Risk Analysis

D. Probability Impact Matrix

☑ **B.** Developing options, determining actions to enhance opportunities, and reducing threats to project objectives is known as Plan Risk Responses.

☒ **A, C,** and **D** are incorrect. **A** and **C** are incorrect because Perform Qualitative Risk Analysis and Perform Quantitative Risk Analysis are prior steps in the Risk Management process. **D** is incorrect because the Probability Impact Matrix is a means of classifying the ranking of risks.

9. Your team is developing a part of the risk management plan. For some of the risks, the team decides that a response plan will be executed only when certain predefined conditions exist. What is the term given to this type of risk strategy?

A. Contingent

B. Sharing

C. Exploit

D. Enhance

☑ **A.** For some of the risks in a project, whether they pose a threat or provide an opportunity, a response plan that will be executed only when certain predefined conditions exist is called a contingent response strategy.

☒ **B**, **C**, and **D** are incorrect. Sharing, exploiting, and enhancing are responses to opportunity related to risk events.

10. Information such as outcomes of risk reassessments, risk audits, and periodic risk reviews are examples from which of the following?

    A. Risk management plan

    B. Approved change requests

    C. Project document updates

    D. Work performance information

    ☑ **C.** Information such as outcomes of risk reassessments, risk audits, and periodic risk reviews are examples of project document updates from the Control Risk process.

    ☒ **A**, **B**, and **D** are incorrect. **A** is incorrect because the risk management plan defines the process and resources involved in managing the risks. **B** and **D** are incorrect because approved change requests and work performance information do not match the question items.

11. As part of implementing risk responses, you are updating your risk report. You should include:

    A. Any changes to overall risk exposure

    B. Impact of identified risks on achieving project benefits

    C. A change request process for risks that occur that affect project team assignments

    D. A revised list of prioritized issues that affect the project's objectives

    ☑ **A.** The risk report may be updated to include changes to overall project risk exposure that occur from the Implement Risk Responses process.

    ☒ **B**, **C**, and **D** are incorrect. **B** is incorrect because the risk register already includes the impact of identified risks on achieving project benefits and was being monitored before implementing the risk response. **C** is incorrect because the question does not mention limiting the risk responses to those that affect project team assignments. **D** is incorrect because the issue log includes a revised list of prioritized issues that affect the project's objectives.

12. In the Implement Risk Responses process, which of the following is done for each risk?

    A. Specify the risk thresholds based on the risk appetite of the sponsor.

    B. Encourage risk owners to take necessary action, if required.

    C. Document the risk description and impact if it happens.

    D. Inform project stakeholders of all ranked risks.

    ☑ **B.** Regardless of the severity of the risk or threshold of risk appetite, every risk has an owner, and each owner is encouraged to take action when necessary whether it is a low-risk item or a high-risk item. No proactive action is taken other than encouraging the owner of the risk to take action at the appropriate time.

☒ **A**, **C**, and **D** are incorrect. **A** is incorrect because specifying the risk thresholds based on the risk appetite of the sponsor is part of planning risk management. **C** is incorrect because you document risks in the risk register, and you inform stakeholders in a risk meeting. **D** is incorrect because even if the risk is a low-priority threat, the risk will still be added to the risk register and monitored in risk meetings.

13. What are you engaged in if you are documenting the effectiveness of risk responses in dealing with identified risks and their root causes, as well as the effectiveness of the risk management process?

    A. Implement risk responses

    B. Risk identification

    C. Risk analysis

    D. Risk audit

    ☑ **D**. The actions of documenting the effectiveness of risk responses in dealing with identified risks and the root causes, and of the effectiveness of the Risk Management process, is known as a risk audit.

    ☒ **A**, **B**, and **C** are incorrect. **A** is incorrect because risk responses are a specific set of alternatives to manage risk. **B** and **C** are incorrect because Risk Identification and Risk Analysis are processes used to build a risk management plan.

14. In which process does a project manager prioritize individual risks by assessing their probability of occurrence and impact?

    A. Plan Risk Management

    B. Identify Risks

    C. Perform Qualitative Risk Analysis

    D. Perform Quantitative Risk Analysis

    ☑ **C**. Within the Project Risk Management processes, it is during the Perform Qualitative Risk Analysis process that the project manager examines the probability that each risk will occur and the associated risk to the project.

    ☒ **A**, **B**, and **D** are incorrect. **A** is incorrect because in Plan Risk Management, the project manager plans an approach to risk that is appropriate to the project. **B** is incorrect because in Identify Risks, the project manager identifies all known risks. **D** is incorrect because in Quantitative Risk Analysis, the project manager numerically analyzes the combined effects of identified individual project risks and other sources of uncertainty on overall project objectives.

15. In which process does the project manager numerically analyze the combined effect of identified individual project risks and other sources of uncertainty on overall project objectives?

    A. Plan Risk Management

    B. Identify Risks

C. Perform Qualitative Risk Analysis

D. Perform Quantitative Risk Analysis

☑ **D.** In Qualitative Risk Analysis, the project manager numerically analyzes the combined effects of identified individual project risks and other sources of uncertainty on overall project objectives.

☒ **A**, **B**, and **C** are incorrect. **A** is incorrect because in Plan Risk Management, the project manager plans an approach to risk that is appropriate to the project. **B** is incorrect because in Identify Risks, the project manager identifies all known risks. **C** is incorrect because in Perform Qualitative Risk Analysis, the project manager examines the probability that each risk will occur and the associated risk to the project.

16. Calculate EMV for a risk event that has a 40 percent chance of occurring and that, if it occurred, would cost the project an additional $100,000.

A. $4,000

B. $40,000

C. $100,000

D. $400,000

☑ **B.** 40% * $100,000 = $40,000. The three steps to calculate EMV are as follows: 1. Assign a probability of occurrence for the risk. 2. Assign a monetary value for the impact of the risk when it occurs. 3. Multiply step 1 and step 2. The value you get after performing step 3 is the expected monetary value. This value is positive for opportunities (positive risks) and negative for threats (negative risks). Project Risk Management requires you to address both types of project risks.

☒ **A**, **C**, and **D** are incorrect. The answers do not come from following the three steps of calculating EMV.

17. Risk A has a 50 percent chance of happening. Unrelated Risk B has a 20 percent chance of happening. What is the chance they will both happen?

A. 10 percent

B. 30 percent

C. 70 percent

D. 100 percent

☑ **A.** 10% because 0.50 * 0.20 = 0.10 = 10% (or 1/2 * 1/5 = 1/10). When two events are independent, the probability of both occurring is the product of the probabilities of the individual events. More formally, if events A and B are independent, then the probability of both A and B occurring is P(A and B) = P(A) × P(B).

☒ **B**, **C**, and **D** are incorrect. They were not arrived at by calculating the probability of two independent events through multiplication of the probabilities of the two events.

18. If the EMV of a risk is $200,000 and this risk exposure has been documented in the project business case, what is the maximum you could spend to remove the risk completely and be better off?

    A. $20,000

    B. $100,000

    C. $2,000,000

    D. $200,000

    ☑ **D.** $200,000. The maximum amount you would spend to eliminate the risk completely is equal to the amount of risk exposure.

    ☒ **A, B,** and **C** are incorrect. **A** and **B** are incorrect because the question asks for the maximum amount you could spend. **C** is incorrect because spending any more than the amount of risk exposure is not a sound project management practice.

19. A residual risk is assessed to have a probability of 0.1 and an impact value of $50,000. What is the EMV of the residual risk?

    A. $1,000

    B. $5,000

    C. $50,000

    D. EMV does not apply to residual risk

    ☑ **B.** $5,000. The three steps to calculate EMV are as follows: 1. Assign a probability of occurrence for the risk. 2. Assign a monetary value for the impact of the risk when it occurs. 3. Multiply step 1 and step 2. The value you get after performing step 3 is the expected monetary value. This value is positive for opportunities (positive risks) and negative for threats (negative risks). Project Risk Management requires you to address both types of project risks.

    ☒ **A, C,** and **D** are incorrect. The answers do not come from following the three steps for calculating EMV.

20. How is secondary risk assessed?

    A. E = (a + 4m + b) / 6

    B. EMV plus 10 percent

    C. Determine probability and multiply by impact

    D. The same way as original or residual risks

    ☑ **D.** Secondary risk is a risk that happens because you implemented a risk response. A residual risk is the risk that remains after a risk response has been taken. Secondary risks should be assessed for proper action in the same way as original risks and residual risks.

    ☒ **A, B,** and **C** are incorrect. **A** is incorrect because it is the formula for three-point estimating. **B** is incorrect because it is an improper calculation. **C** is incorrect because it is the definition of risk exposure.

21. In order to prepare the risk management plan, what should a project manager define first?

   A. Your organization's risk appetite

   B. The functional requirements document you plan to use to identify risks

   C. The resisting stakeholders

   D. Budget assumptions and constraints

   ☑ **A.** In risk management, risk appetite is the level of risk an organization is prepared to accept. Risk appetite constraints are not easy to define; every organization can tolerate different levels of risk.

   ☒ **B, C,** and **D** are incorrect. **B** is incorrect because the functional requirements document may indicate project objectives that are particularly at risk and is an input to the risk management plan. **C** is incorrect because a resistant stakeholder will be identified in the stakeholder engagement assessment matrix in the stakeholder management plan. **D** is incorrect because budget assumptions and constraints will be used to keep the known risks within the identified risk thresholds.

22. You are preparing to lead a project team creating a product that is expected to be available for the Christmas buying season and is anticipated to be popular with young adults ages 25 to 35. What should you be sure to review before finalizing the risk management plan for this particular project?

   A. Occupational safety and health issues

   B. Business case

   C. Potential suppliers on the prequalified sellers list

   D. Cultural differences in the production workers

   ☑ **B.** When managing risk, market factors that apply to the project should be included as an enterprise environmental factor. Market demand, a high risk, is included in the business case.

   ☒ **A, C,** and **D** are incorrect. **A** is incorrect because although you will comply with OSHA regulations in your new building, it is a relatively low risk compared to no market for your gadgets. **C** is incorrect because the question does not imply the use of potential sellers. **D** is incorrect because resource (production workers) risks are known risks and are mitigated later in the risk management processes.

23. You have a design team of seven members and a support team of three people; these numbers are about half of what you believe you need. These limits are examples of:

   A. Constraints to document in your project scope statement

   B. Limitations to document in your project charter

   C. Known risks to set aside management reserves

   D. Key issues to document in the risk log

   ☑ **A.** These are examples of constraints. Constraints and assumptions should be included in the scope statement.

☒ **B**, **C**, and **D** are incorrect. **B** is incorrect because resource limitations are not documented in the project charter. High-level boundaries are listed in the project charter. **C** is incorrect because contingency reserves are set aside for known risks. Unknown risks are covered by management reserves. Risks are documented in the risk register. **D** is incorrect because key issues are documented in the issues log.

24. A generally accepted business practice to follow regarding risks and issues is to:

    A. Use the risk register to capture operational-level issues

    B. Set up a risk control board for risks and issues that may occur

    C. Set up an escalation process for you to help resolve risks and issues

    D. Ensure a risk or issue is isolated to a single project phase

    ☑ **C.** Risks or issues related to project objectives, resource and intergroup conflicts, ambiguous roles and responsibilities, scope disagreements, and third-party dependencies are some known situations calling for escalation. Such issues require higher-level intervention because many times the authority, decision making, resources, or effort required to resolve them is beyond a project manager's scope.

    ☒ **A**, **B**, and **D** are incorrect. **A** is incorrect because issues are recorded in the issues log, not the risk register. **B** is incorrect because although there is a change control board, there is not a separate risk control board. Risks are evaluated by the change control board during an impact assessment. **D** is incorrect because the risk management processes identify risks by category and select risk strategies to address overall risk exposure throughout the project, including when risks and issues span project phases.

Project Procurement Management

In this chapter, you will

- Understand the three processes in the Project Procurement Management knowledge area
- Identify the inputs, tools, techniques, and outputs defined in the three project procurement processes
- Identify key concepts and tailoring considerations for Project Procurement Management, including trends and emerging practices
- Identify various types of contracts, agreements, and source selection methods

The Project Procurement Management knowledge area accounts for 4 percent (12) of the questions on the CAPM exam. The *PMBOK Guide, Sixth Edition,* Sections 12.1 through 12.3, cover the three processes in the Project Procurement Management knowledge area.

This chapter focuses on the topic of Project Procurement Management, which, like the other knowledge areas, begins with a process of planning, which in this case produces a procurement management plan. It then uses this plan to carry out the procurement work, which involves making decisions about whether to procure goods, services, or resources from external sources and, if so, how to advertise and award the contract and what form of contract to use. Procurement management also involves monitoring contractual terms for performance and includes making sure all contracts are formally closed.

The 12 practice questions in this chapter are mapped to the style and frequency of question types you will see on the CAPM exam.

1. Which of the following processes produces the procurement management plan?

    A. Close Procurements

    B. Plan Procurement Management

    C. Conduct Procurements

    D. Develop Procurement Management Plan

2. The organization seeking to procure external resources to provide goods or services on a project is known as what?

    A. Procurement specialist

    B. Seller

    C. Lawyer

    D. Buyer

3. You are the seller of a potential good or service and are responding to an RFP document where there is a poorly defined scope of work. What type of contract would you prefer to enter?

    A. Fixed-price

    B. Fixed price incentive fee

    C. Cost-reimbursable

    D. Time and materials

4. The document that describes and defines the portion of the project scope to be included within the related contract is known as what?

    A. Procurement management plan

    B. Organizational process assets

    C. Scope statement

    D. Procurement statement of work

5. A technique that considers a variety of factors to determine whether the particular project work is best done by the project team or done by external sources is known as what?

    A. Expert judgment

    B. Market research

    C. Make-or-buy analysis

    D. Proposal evaluation techniques

6. All the following could be included as part of your source selection criteria except what?

   A. Intellectual property rights

   B. Technical capability

   C. Financial capacity

   D. Organizational process assets

7. You have decided to engage the services of a quantity surveyor to review the prices received from sellers responding to your procurement requests. What tool or technique are you using?

   A. Delphi technique

   B. Independent estimates

   C. Analytical techniques

   D. Bidder conferences

8. You and your team are in the process of negotiating a contract for a service required on your project. Which process are you in?

   A. Plan Procurement Management

   B. Conduct Procurements

   C. Control Procurements

   D. Close Contracts

9. Who is responsible for carrying out audits on contracts?

   A. Only the buyer

   B. Only the seller

   C. An independent legal professional

   D. Both buyer and seller

10. Which tool or technique would be most useful for storing information about procurement documentation and records?

    A. Records management system

    B. Project management information system

    C. Contract change control system

    D. Procurement performance reviews

11. All the following conditions can lead to early termination of a contract except what?

   A. Mutual agreement by both parties

   B. Default of one party

   C. Convenience of the buyer if provided for in the contract

   D. An incomplete procurement statement of work

12. Which of the following is not a form of alternative dispute resolution?

   A. Mediation

   B. Arbitration

   C. Litigation

   D. Audit

1. B	**5.** C	**9.** D
2. D	**6.** D	**10.** A
3. D	**7.** B	**11.** D
4. D	**8.** B	**12.** D

1. Which of the following processes produces the procurement management plan?

   A. Close Procurements

   B. Plan Procurement Management

   C. Conduct Procurements

   D. Develop Procurement Management Plan

   ☑ **B**. The Plan Procurement Management process has the procurement management plan as its primary output.

   ☒ **A**, **C**, and **D** are incorrect. **A** is incorrect because the Close Procurements process is a name from the *PMBOK Guide, Fifth Edition*, and was the process that closed contracts after they had been fulfilled. **C** is incorrect because Conduct Procurements uses the procurement management plan. **D** is incorrect because Develop Procurement Management Plan is a made-up process name.

2. The organization seeking to procure external resources to provide goods or services on a project is known as what?

   A. Procurement specialist

   B. Seller

   C. Lawyer

   D. Buyer

   ☑ **D**. The buyer is the organization that is requiring goods or services to be performed and is asking for external sources to do the work via a negotiated contract.

   ☒ **A**, **B**, and **C** are incorrect. **A** is incorrect because the procurement specialist may be an expert that you choose to use as part of your decision to procure from external sources. **B** is incorrect because the seller is the organization or individual who is responding to a request from a buyer for the provision of goods and services. **C** is incorrect because a lawyer can act for either buyer or seller.

3. You are the seller of a potential good or service and are responding to an RFP document where there is a poorly defined scope of work. What type of contract would you prefer to enter?

   A. Fixed-price

   B. Fixed price incentive fee

   C. Cost-reimbursable

   D. Time and materials

   ☑ **D**. Given that there is a poorly defined scope of work, you want to enter into the type of contract that represents the least risk to you, the seller, which is a time and materials contract.

☒ **A**, **B**, and **C** are incorrect. **A** is incorrect because a fixed-price contract would represent the greatest risk to the seller in the face of a poorly defined scope of work. **B** is incorrect because a fixed price incentive fee contract does little to remove the risk to the seller with a poorly defined scope of work. **C** is incorrect because a cost-reimbursable form of contract may be preferable to a fixed-price form of contract where there is a poorly defined scope of work, but it still represents more risk to the seller than a time and materials contract.

4. The document that describes and defines the portion of the project scope to be included within the related contract is known as what?

    A. Procurement management plan

    B. Organizational process assets

    C. Scope statement

    D. Procurement statement of work

    ☑ **D.** The procurement statement of work describes and defines the portion of the project scope to be completed as part of a negotiated contract.

    ☒ **A**, **B**, and **C** are incorrect. **A** is incorrect because the procurement management plan provides guidelines for carrying out the entire procurement management process. **B** is incorrect because organizational process assets include templates, historical information, and other guidelines of use in carrying out the procurement management process, but they do not describe or define the work to be done as part of the contract. **C** is incorrect because the project scope statement defines and describes all the work to be done as part of the project; the procurement statement of work is a subset of the project scope statement specifically related to the work to be done as part of a contract.

5. A technique that considers a variety of factors to determine whether the particular project work is best done by the project team or done by external sources is known as what?

    A. Expert judgment

    B. Market research

    C. Make-or-buy analysis

    D. Proposal evaluation techniques

    ☑ **C.** Make-or-buy analysis is the technique that considers a variety of factors to determine whether you should complete the work in-house or outsource it.

    ☒ **A**, **B**, and **D** are incorrect. **A** is incorrect because expert judgment is used as a tool and may contribute to the make-or-buy analysis, but it is not the best answer. **B** is incorrect because market research is a technique that examines the number of potential sellers and their interest in responding to your procurement documents. **D** is incorrect because proposal evaluation techniques are used after sellers have responded to your requests in order to determine which sellers advance in the procurement process.

6. All the following could be included as part of your source selection criteria except what?

   A. Intellectual property rights

   B. Technical capability

   C. Financial capacity

   D. Organizational process assets

   ☑ **D**. Organizational process assets may help you with the procurement management processes, but they would not be included as part of your source selection criteria.

   ☒ **A**, **B**, and **C** are incorrect. **A** is incorrect because intellectual property rights are an important consideration in your source selection criteria to determine who ultimately owns the work performed as part of a contract. **B** is incorrect because technical capability will be considered as part of your source selection criteria to ensure that the selected seller has the technical capability to perform the required work. **C** is incorrect because financial capacity will be considered as part of your source selection criteria to ensure that the sellers chosen are of sufficient financial strength and stability to be able to complete the work.

7. You have decided to engage the services of a quantity surveyor to review the prices received from sellers responding to your procurement requests. What tool or technique are you using?

   A. Delphi technique

   B. Independent estimates

   C. Analytical techniques

   D. Bidder conferences

   ☑ **B**. Independent estimates are a technique used to determine if prices received from sellers are accurate.

   ☒ **A**, **C**, and **D** are incorrect. **A** is incorrect because the Delphi technique is a tool used to solicit information from participants anonymously to reach consensus. **C** is incorrect because analytical techniques are a particular tool used to evaluate a variety of elements and seller responses, not just price. **D** is incorrect because bidder conferences are used to provide information to prospective sellers on a fair and equitable basis.

8. You and your team are in the process of negotiating a contract for a service required on your project. Which process are you in?

   A. Plan Procurement Management

   B. Conduct Procurements

   C. Control Procurements

   D. Close Contracts

   ☑ **B**. The Conduct Procurements process uses the project management plan and seeks to negotiate contracts with potential sellers.

☒ **A, C**, and **D** are incorrect. **A** is incorrect because the Plan Procurement Management process is focused on the production of the procurement management plan and procurement statement of work, which will assist with the Conduct Procurements process, during which contracts are negotiated. **C** is incorrect because the Control Procurements process monitors the negotiated contracts but does not actually negotiate them. **D** is incorrect because Close Contracts is a made-up term.

9. Who is responsible for carrying out audits on contracts?

   A. Only the buyer

   B. Only the seller

   C. An independent legal professional

   D. Both buyer and seller

   ☑ **D.** Both buyer and seller are responsible for carrying out audits on contracts, because they are both parties to the contract and have responsibilities under the negotiated terms and conditions.

   ☒ **A, B**, and **C** are incorrect. **A** is incorrect because the seller is also responsible for carrying out audits on contracts to ensure that both they and the buyer are meeting the agreed-to terms and conditions. **B** is incorrect because the buyer also has responsibility for carrying out audits of the contracts because they initiated the process and have obligations as well. **C** is incorrect because an independent legal professional may be engaged by either buyer or seller, but the ultimate responsibility lies with both buyer and seller.

10. Which tool or technique would be most useful for storing information about procurement documentation and records?

    A. Records management system

    B. Project management information system

    C. Contract change control system

    D. Procurement performance reviews

    ☑ **A.** The records management system is a subset of the project management information system devoted to storing information about procurement documentation and records.

    ☒ **B, C**, and **D** are incorrect. **B** is incorrect because the project management information system includes the records management system, which is the better answer to this question because it specifically focuses upon storing information about procurement documentation and records. **C** is incorrect because the contract change control system records information about requested contractual changes and the status. **D** is incorrect because procurement performance reviews gather information about whether each party to a contract is carrying out their obligations and responsibilities. Information gathered from procurement performance reviews will be stored in a records management system.

11. All the following conditions can lead to early termination of a contract except what?

   A. Mutual agreement by both parties

   B. Default of one party

   C. Convenience of the buyer if provided for in the contract

   D. An incomplete procurement statement of work

   ☑ **D**. An incomplete procurement statement of work may lead to disagreements, change requests, and claims but not generally to an early termination of the contract except under extreme circumstances.

   ☒ **A, B**, and **C** are incorrect. **A** is incorrect because both parties can, by way of mutual agreement, agree to terminate the contract early. **B** is incorrect because the default of one party to a contract is considered sufficient cause for early termination of a contract. **C** is incorrect because some forms of contracts have written into them that early termination can occur if it is convenient to the buyer. These contracts normally include some form of compensation to the seller.

12. Which of the following is not a form of alternative dispute resolution?

   A. Mediation

   B. Arbitration

   C. Litigation

   D. Audit

   ☑ **D**. An audit is used to determine whether parties to a contract are carrying the contract out as per the agreed-to terms and conditions.

   ☒ **A, B**, and **C** are incorrect. **A** is incorrect because mediation is a form of alternative dispute resolution that seeks to reach an agreement with both parties. **B** is incorrect because arbitration is a form of alternative dispute resolution that brings in a third party to make a decision that is binding on both parties. **C** is incorrect because litigation is a form of alternative dispute resolution that involves some form of court involvement.

Project Stakeholder Management

In this chapter, you will

- Understand the four project management processes in the Project Stakeholder Management knowledge area
- Identify the inputs, tools, techniques, and outputs defined in the four Project Stakeholder Management processes
- Recognize key stakeholders roles and needs
- Identify the key concepts and benefits of stakeholder management

One of the most interesting aspects of a project is that every project has multiple stakeholders and each stakeholder group acts according to their own objectives. Identifying all the right stakeholders and engaging stakeholders early and often and managing the continuous communication with stakeholders are critical to the success of both the project manager and the project: Stakeholder satisfaction is at the core of project success. The four processes within Project Stakeholder Management emphasize capturing and maintaining stakeholder interest and keeping the stakeholders and what they value clearly on the project manager radar screen.

The 27 practice questions in this chapter are mapped to the style and frequency of question types you will see on the CAPM exam.

1. Which process results in the initial creation of a project stakeholder register?

    A. Identify Stakeholders

    B. Manage Stakeholder Engagement

    C. Monitor Stakeholder Engagement

    D. Plan Stakeholder Management

2. Which process group contains the Identify Stakeholders process?

    A. Initiating

    B. Planning

    C. Executing

    D. Monitoring and Controlling

3. Which Project Stakeholder Management process has the goal of working with stakeholders to meet their needs and expectations?

    A. Identify Stakeholders

    B. Manage Stakeholder Engagement

    C. Monitor Stakeholder Engagement

    D. Plan Stakeholder Management

4. Which process puts emphasis on communicating with stakeholders?

    A. Identify Stakeholders

    B. Manage Stakeholder Engagement

    C. Monitor Stakeholder Engagement

    D. Plan Stakeholder Management

5. Which of the following is a true statement regarding the Project Stakeholder Management processes?

    A. The processes are carried out independent of one another.

    B. All of the processes focus on communication with stakeholders.

    C. All of the processes are carried out in the Initiating Process Group.

    D. The processes overlap and interact with one another.

6. Which project document is completed just before the process of Identify Stakeholders takes place?

    A. Business case

    B. Project charter

    C. Project plan

    D. Stakeholder register

7. What is the goal of developing approaches to involve stakeholders in the Plan Stakeholder Engagement process?

    A. Base the approach on project goals.

    B. Base the approach on the project sponsor's goals and objectives.

    C. Base the approach on stakeholder needs and expectations.

    D. Base the approach on the project team's needs of the stakeholders.

8. Which two processes require that the Project Charter be completed first?

    A. Identify Stakeholders and Plan Stakeholder Engagement

    B. Plan Stakeholder Engagement and Manage Stakeholder Engagement

    C. Manage Stakeholder Engagement and Monitor Stakeholder Engagement

    D. Plan Stakeholder Engagement and Monitor Stakeholder Engagement

9. Which Project Stakeholder Management process sets ground rules as one of its tools and techniques?

    A. Identify Stakeholders

    B. Manage Stakeholder Engagement

    C. Monitor Stakeholder Engagement

    D. Plan Stakeholder Management

10. Which Project Stakeholder Management process creates work performance information as an output?

    A. Identify Stakeholders

    B. Manage Stakeholder Engagement

    C. Monitor Stakeholder Engagement

    D. Plan Stakeholder Management

11. Questionnaires, surveys, brainstorming, and benchmarking are examples of which technique?

    A. Expert judgment

    B. Data gathering

    C. Data analysis

    D. Decision-making

12. If you are identifying the underlying reasons why project stakeholders are not engaged in the project, what type of technique and which technique are you using?

    A. Expert judgment – Delphi

    B. Data gathering – Surveys

    C. Data analysis – Root-cause analysis

    D. Data representation – Stakeholder engagement assessment matrix

13. If you are allocating stakeholders into categories of unaware, resistant, neutral, supportive, or leading, which technique type and which technique are you using?

   A. Expert judgment – Delphi

   B. Data gathering – Surveys

   C. Data analysis – Root-cause analysis

   D. Data representation – Stakeholder engagement assessment matrix

14. If you are using work performance data and updating the issue log project document while clarifying and resolving issues identified by stakeholders, which process are you carrying out?

   A. Identify Stakeholders

   B. Manage Stakeholder Engagement

   C. Monitor Stakeholder Engagement

   D. Plan Stakeholder Management

15. In an adaptive environment using the processes of Project Stakeholder Management, which stakeholder roles often exchange information in a co-creative way?

   A. Client, user, and developer

   B. Project manager, business analyst, and QA manager

   C. Project sponsor, project manager, and QA manager

   D. Project sponsor, the PMO, and the project manager

16. Which technique describes classes of stakeholders based on assessments of their level of authority, urgency, and legitimacy?

   A. Stakeholder cube

   B. Salience model

   C. Directions of influence

   D. Prioritization

17. What is the recommended project size for working with the power/interest, power/influence, and impact/influence grids?

   A. Small projects

   B. Medium projects

   C. Large projects

   D. All projects

18. Which project document contains any constraints associated with specific stakeholders and interacting with them?

   A. Assumption log

   B. Issue log

C. Risk register

D. Stakeholder register

19. Which of the following describes the influence of stakeholders on the work of the project if the stakeholder group is the project team?

   A. Upward

   B. Downward

   C. Outward

   D. Sideward

20. If you classify a stakeholder's engagement as "leading," what is true of this stakeholder?

   A. The stakeholder is unaware of the project and potential impacts.

   B. The stakeholder is unsupportive of the project work or the project outcomes.

   C. The stakeholder is aware of the project and supportive of project work and outcomes.

   D. The stakeholder is actively engaged in ensuring the project is a success.

21. Which of the following interpersonal and team skills is used to understand power relationships within and around the project?

   A. Conflict management

   B. Cultural awareness

   C. Observation/conversation

   D. Political awareness

22. Why should a project manager put emphasis on the Project Stakeholder Management processes?

   A. To integrate the team with the stakeholder groups

   B. To allow the stakeholders to guide the project decisions

   C. To increase the possibility that stakeholders will attend to project details

   D. To increase the chance of project success

23. What is recommended in order to understand stakeholder needs and expectations, issue management, and overall stakeholder engagement in a project?

   A. Fully developed WBS

   B. Including a business analyst in the Executing phase of a project

   C. Continuous communication

   D. Incorporating a dedicated testing group during Monitoring and Controlling

24. What is a key benefit of the Identify Stakeholders process?

    A. Enables the project team to identify the appropriate level of engagement for each stakeholder group

    B. Enables the project manager to assign the project team to the appropriate stakeholder group

    C. Enables the project sponsor to visualize the best way to allocate resources to the project

    D. Enables the project manager to design an effective matrix management approach

25. Which project process or document is updated iteratively to coincide with updates needed as a result of the work taking place in the project?

    A. Modifying the project charter

    B. Updating the procurement contracts

    C. Tailoring the SWOT analysis

    D. Identifying project stakeholders

26. When should the process of stakeholder identification engagement start in order to increase the chance of project success?

    A. As soon as possible after approving the project plan

    B. As soon as possible after approving the project charter

    C. As soon as possible after completing the RACI chart

    D. As soon as possible after completing the risk register

27. Which project document is initiated then updated with details on project participants, including their expectations?

    A. Requirements documentation

    B. Stakeholder register

    C. Risk register

    D. Project team assignments

1. A	**10.** C	**19.** B
2. A	**11.** B	**20.** D
3. B	**12.** C	**21.** D
4. B	**13.** D	**22.** D
5. D	**14.** C	**23.** C
6. B	**15.** A	**24.** A
7. C	**16.** B	**25.** D
8. A	**17.** A	**26.** B
9. B	**18.** A	**27.** B

1. Which process results in the initial creation of a project stakeholder register?

   A. Identify Stakeholders

   B. Manage Stakeholder Engagement

   C. Monitor Stakeholder Engagement

   D. Plan Stakeholder Management

   ☑ **A.** The stakeholder register is an output of the Identify Stakeholders process.

   ☒ **B, C,** and **D** are incorrect. Although the stakeholder register may be updated through the life of a project, its initial creation takes place in Identify Stakeholders, which is part of the Initiating process group.

2. Which process group contains the Identify Stakeholders process?

   A. Initiating

   B. Planning

   C. Executing

   D. Monitoring and Controlling

   ☑ **A.** The Identify Stakeholders process is part of the Initiating process group directly after Develop Project Charter.

   ☒ **B, C,** and **D.** The Identify Stakeholders process appears as part of the Initiating process group. Even though it is not shown in Planning, Executing, or Monitoring and Controlling, the Identify Stakeholders process is considered to overlap across the entire project and all process groups.

3. Which Project Stakeholder Management process has the goal of working with stakeholders to meet their needs and expectations?

   A. Identify Stakeholders

   B. Manage Stakeholder Engagement

   C. Monitor Stakeholder Engagement

   D. Plan Stakeholder Management

   ☑ **B.** Manage Stakeholder Engagement is about working with stakeholders to meet their needs and expectations.

   ☒ **A, C,** and **D** are incorrect. **A** is incorrect because Identify Stakeholders focuses on identifying project stakeholders iteratively. **C** is incorrect because Monitor Stakeholder Engagement focuses on understanding relationships and tailoring engagement approaches. **D** is incorrect because Plan Stakeholder Management focuses on developing involvement strategies for stakeholders.

4. Which process puts emphasis on communicating with stakeholders?

   A. Identify Stakeholders

   B. Manage Stakeholder Engagement

   C. Monitor Stakeholder Engagement

   D. Plan Stakeholder Management

   ☑ **B**. Manage Stakeholder Engagement is about communicating throughout the project with stakeholders.

   ☒ **A, C**, and **D** are incorrect. **A** is incorrect because Identify Stakeholders focuses on identifying project stakeholders iteratively. **C** is incorrect because Monitor Stakeholder Engagement focuses on understanding relationships and tailoring engagement approaches. **D** is incorrect because Plan Stakeholder Management focuses on developing involvement strategies for stakeholders.

5. Which of the following is a true statement regarding the Project Stakeholder Management processes?

   A. The processes are carried out independent of one another.

   B. All of the processes focus on communication with stakeholders.

   C. All of the processes are carried out in the Initiating Process Group.

   D. The processes overlap and interact with one another.

   ☑ **D** is correct because even though each process appears once in the *PMBOK Guide* and they are presented as discrete processes with defined interfaces, in practice, the processes overlap and interact.

   ☒ **A, B**, and **C** are incorrect. **A** is incorrect because the processes overlap. **B** is incorrect because Manage Stakeholder Engagement is about communicating throughout the project with stakeholders. **C** is incorrect because only Identify Stakeholders takes place in the Initiating Process Group.

6. Which project document is completed just before the process of Identify Stakeholders takes place?

   A. Business case

   B. Project charter

   C. Project plan

   D. Stakeholder register

   ☑ **B**. As soon as the project charter is complete, the process of Identify Stakeholders should start.

   ☒ **A, C**, and **D** are incorrect. The process of Identify Stakeholders is dependent on the project charter being complete in the Initiating process group. **A** is incorrect because the business case precedes the project charter. **C** is incorrect because the project plan will not be complete until into the Planning process group. **D** is incorrect because the stakeholder register is started after the Identify Stakeholders process.

7. What is the goal of developing approaches to involve stakeholders in the Plan Stakeholder Engagement process?

   A. Base the approach on project goals.

   B. Base the approach on the project sponsor's goals and objectives.

   C. Base the approach on stakeholder needs and expectations.

   D. Base the approach on the project team's needs of the stakeholders.

   ☑ **C.** The goal of the Plan Stakeholder Engagement process focuses on stakeholder needs and expectations.

   ☒ **A, B,** and **D** are incorrect. Stakeholder needs and expectations are the focus of Plan Stakeholder Engagement and not the goals of the project, sponsor, or project team.

8. Which two processes require that the Project Charter be completed first?

   A. Identify Stakeholders and Plan Stakeholder Engagement

   B. Plan Stakeholder Engagement and Manage Stakeholder Engagement

   C. Manage Stakeholder Engagement and Monitor Stakeholder Engagement

   D. Plan Stakeholder Engagement and Monitor Stakeholder Engagement

   ☑ **A.** Identify Stakeholders and Plan Stakeholder Engagement both have the project charter as an input.

   ☒ **B, C,** and **D** are incorrect. Identify Stakeholders and Plan Stakeholder Engagement both have the project charter as an input, whereas neither Manage Stakeholder Engagement nor Monitor Stakeholder Engagement have the project charter as an input.

9. Which Project Stakeholder Management process sets ground rules as one of its tools and techniques?

   A. Identify Stakeholders

   B. Manage Stakeholder Engagement

   C. Monitor Stakeholder Engagement

   D. Plan Stakeholder Management

   ☑ **B.** The Manage Stakeholder Engagement process has ground rules as a tool and technique. Ground rules set the expected behavior for team members relative to stakeholder engagement.

   ☒ **A, C,** and **D** are incorrect. Only the Manage Stakeholder Engagement process has ground rules as a tool and technique. In fact, no other process mentions ground rules as a technique.

10. Which Project Stakeholder Management process creates work performance information as an output?

    A. Identify Stakeholders

    B. Manage Stakeholder Engagement

    C. Monitor Stakeholder Engagement

    D. Plan Stakeholder Management

    ☑ **C.** The Monitor Stakeholder Engagement process takes work performance data as an input and transforms it to create work performance information. Examples include status of deliverables and implementation status for change requests.

    ☒ **A**, **B**, and **D** are incorrect. Only the Monitor Stakeholder Engagement process in the Plan Stakeholder Management process group creates work performance information.

11. Questionnaires, surveys, brainstorming, and benchmarking are examples of which technique?

    A. Expert judgment

    B. Data gathering

    C. Data analysis

    D. Decision-making

    ☑ **B.** Questionnaires, surveys, brainstorming, and benchmarking demonstrate data-gathering techniques useful in many process groups.

    ☒ **A**, **C**, and **D** are incorrect. **A** is incorrect because expert judgment is not strictly a data-gathering technique and is used in every process in all process groups. **C** and **D** are incorrect because data analysis and decision-making take place after data-gathering techniques like questionnaires, surveys, brainstorming, and benchmarking.

12. If you are identifying the underlying reasons why project stakeholders are not engaged in the project, what type of technique and which technique are you using?

    A. Expert judgment – Delphi

    B. Data gathering – Surveys

    C. Data analysis – Root-cause analysis

    D. Data representation – Stakeholder engagement assessment matrix

    ☑ **C** is correct. Identifying the underlying reasons for a problem is called root-cause analysis and is a part of data analysis.

    ☒ **A**, **B**, and **D** are incorrect. The question asks about identifying the underlying causes for a problem, which is root-cause analysis and is not expert judgment, data gathering, or data representation.

13. If you are allocating stakeholders into categories of unaware, resistant, neutral, supportive, or leading, which technique type and which technique are you using?

  A. Expert judgment – Delphi

  B. Data gathering – Surveys

  C. Data analysis – Root-cause analysis

  D. Data representation – Stakeholder engagement assessment matrix

  ☑ **D.** The data representation stakeholder engagement assessment matrix tracks five stakeholder engagement levels with five categories: unaware, resistant, neutral, supportive, and leading. These categories are tracked to compare the current engagement level of the stakeholder and the desired engagement level.

  ☒ **A, B,** and **C** are incorrect. **A** is incorrect because the Delphi expert judgment technique is about seeking varying opinions on a topic. **B** is incorrect because the data-gathering technique of surveys is about collecting raw data on a topic. **C** is incorrect because the data analysis technique of root-cause analysis is about finding underlying issues in a problem being studied.

14. If you are using work performance data and updating the issue log project document while clarifying and resolving issues identified by stakeholders, which process are you carrying out?

  A. Identify Stakeholders

  B. Manage Stakeholder Engagement

  C. Monitor Stakeholder Engagement

  D. Plan Stakeholder Management

  ☑ **C.** Work performance data is an input to the Monitor Stakeholder Engagement process, and outputs of the process include work performance information and project management plan updates.

  ☒ **A, B,** and **D** are incorrect. None of the processes of Identify Stakeholders, Manage Stakeholder Engagement, and Plan Stakeholder Management include work performance data as an input and work performance information as an output.

15. In an adaptive environment using the processes of Project Stakeholder Management, which stakeholder roles often exchange information in a co-creative way?

  A. Client, user, and developer

  B. Project manager, business analyst, and QA manager

  C. Project sponsor, project manager, and QA manager

  D. Project sponsor, the PMO, and the project manager

  ☑ **A.** Agile teams rely on the very close interactions between the client, users, and developers to co-create a solution that deploys a workable product quickly.

☒ **B**, **C**, and **D** are incorrect. The project sponsor, the project manager, and the QA manager are not the key collaborators in an agile team; rather, the focus is on the co-creative process between the client, the users, and the developers.

16. Which technique describes classes of stakeholders based on assessments of their level of authority, urgency, and legitimacy?

    A. Stakeholder cube

    B. Salience model

    C. Directions of influence

    D. Prioritization

    ☑ **B**. The salience model allows the analysis of a stakeholder based on the stakeholder's level of authority or ability to influence the outcomes of a project, as well as their need for immediacy and their appropriate involvement (legitimacy) in the project.

    ☒ **A**, **C**, and **D** are incorrect. The techniques of stakeholder cube, directions of influence, and prioritization do not directly examine the three variables of power, urgency, and legitimacy like the salience model.

17. What is the recommended project size for working with the power/interest, power/influence, and impact/influence grids?

    A. Small projects

    B. Medium projects

    C. Large projects

    D. All projects

    ☑ **A**. The recommendation for the 2 × 2 matrix approach of power/interest, power/influence, or impact/influence grids is most appropriate in small projects where there is not a large number of stakeholder groups with complex relationships between the groups and the project.

    ☒ **B**, **C**, and **D** are incorrect. Small projects with simple relationships between stakeholder groups and the project are best served with the 2 × 2 matrix approach of power/interest, power/influence, or impact/influence grids.

18. Which project document contains any constraints associated with specific stakeholders and interacting with them?

    A. Assumption log

    B. Issue log

    C. Risk register

    D. Stakeholder register

    ☑ **A**. The assumption log is where any assumptions or constraints related to a stakeholder group are tracked, which provides a basis for understanding things to be aware of and how to interact with the stakeholder group.

☒ **B**, **C**, and **D** are incorrect. **B** is incorrect because the issue log tracks the status of project issues. **C** is incorrect because the risk register identifies project risks and their mitigation strategies. **D** is incorrect because the stakeholder register tracks identification information, assessment information, and classifications of stakeholders on a project.

19. Which of the following describes the influence of stakeholders on the work of the project if the stakeholder group is the project team?

    A. Upward

    B. Downward

    C. Outward

    D. Sideward

    ☑ **B**. In the direction of influence model, the classification of downward describes the team or team specialists.

    ☒ **A**, **C**, and **D** are incorrect. **A** is incorrect because in the direction of influence model, upward describes senior management of the performing organization or customer organization, sponsor, and steering committee. **C** is incorrect because outward describes stakeholder groups and their representatives. **D** is incorrect because sideward describes peers of the project manager.

20. If you classify a stakeholder's engagement as "leading," what is true of this stakeholder?

    A. The stakeholder is unaware of the project and potential impacts.

    B. The stakeholder is unsupportive of the project work or the project outcomes.

    C. The stakeholder is aware of the project and supportive of project work and outcomes.

    D. The stakeholder is actively engaged in ensuring the project is a success.

    ☑ **D**. In the stakeholder engagement assessment matrix, the "leading" designation means that the stakeholder is aware of the project and the project's potential impacts and is actively engaged in positioning the project for success.

    ☒ **A**, **B**, and **C** are incorrect. **A** is incorrect because a classification of "unaware" means the stakeholder is unaware of the project and potential impacts. **B** is incorrect because a classification of "resistant" means the stakeholder is unsupportive of the project work or the project outcomes. **C** is incorrect because a classification of "neutral" means the stakeholder is aware of the project and supportive of project work and outcomes.

21. Which of the following interpersonal and team skills is used to understand power relationships within and around the project?

    A. Conflict management

    B. Cultural awareness

    C. Observation/conversation

    D. Political awareness

☑ **D**. Political awareness of the project environment is possible only through the understanding of power relationships within and around the project.

☒ **A**, **B**, and **C** are incorrect. **A** is incorrect because conflict management deals with a conflict that has surfaced and must be dealt with. **B** is incorrect because cultural awareness speaks to understanding the different operating styles of organizations. **C** is incorrect because observation/conversation are about staying in touch with stakeholders during a project.

22. Why should a project manager put emphasis on the Project Stakeholder Management processes?

    A. To integrate the team with the stakeholder groups

    B. To allow the stakeholders to guide the project decisions

    C. To increase the possibility that stakeholders will attend to project details

    D. To increase the chance of project success

    ☑ **D**. The ability of the project manager and the project team to identify and engage all project stakeholders can mean the difference between project success and project failure.

    ☒ **A**, **B**, and **C** are incorrect. **A** is incorrect because integrating the team with the stakeholder groups is not the goal. **B** is incorrect because allowing stakeholders to guide the project decisions is not the goal. **C** is incorrect because increasing the possibility that stakeholders will attend to project details is not the goal, although this could be a side effect of good stakeholder management. Stakeholder involvement is critical to project success, and that's why a good project manager emphasizes it.

23. What is recommended in order to understand stakeholder needs and expectations, issue management, and overall stakeholder engagement in a project?

    A. Fully developed WBS

    B. Including a business analyst in the Executing phase of a project

    C. Continuous communication

    D. Incorporating a dedicated testing group during Monitoring and Controlling

    ☑ **C**. Continuous communication is the key to effective stakeholder engagement, including knowing their needs, expectations, and issues and being able to gauge their level of engagement.

    ☒ **A**, **B**, and **D** are incorrect. **A** is incorrect because a fully developed WBS will help manage the project but not necessarily the stakeholder engagement. **B** is incorrect because including a business analyst in all phases (not just Executing) will help the project. **D** is incorrect because incorporating a dedicated testing group during Monitoring and Controlling may not be appropriate, given the size of the project.

24. What is a key benefit of the Identify Stakeholders process?

    A. Enables the project team to identify the appropriate level of engagement for each stakeholder group

    B. Enables the project manager to assign the project team to the appropriate stakeholder group

    C. Enables the project sponsor to visualize the best way to allocate resources to the project

    D. Enables the project manager to design an effective matrix management approach

    ☑ A. Identifying and analyzing stakeholders' needs allows the team to determine and abide by the appropriate level of engagement for each stakeholder group.

    ☒ B, C, and D are incorrect. B is incorrect because a project manager does not assign project team members to stakeholders. C is incorrect because the project sponsor does not allocate project resources. D is incorrect because even though a project exists in a matrix organization or a functional organization, the project manager does not design either.

25. Which project process or document is updated iteratively to coincide with updates needed as a result of the work taking place in the project?

    A. Modifying the project charter

    B. Updating the procurement contracts

    C. Tailoring the SWOT analysis

    D. Identifying project stakeholders

    ☑ D. The stakeholder register is included in the set of project documents for the Project Stakeholder Management processes as an input that also is shown as project document outputs.

    ☒ A, B, and C are incorrect. A is incorrect because the project charter is not updated after it is created for the Initiating process. B is incorrect because procurement contracts would not be updated as a part of the Project Stakeholder Management processes. C is incorrect because a SWOT analysis is a type of analysis and is not an input or output of the processes.

26. When should the process of stakeholder identification engagement start in order to increase the chance of project success?

    A. As soon as possible after approving the project plan

    B. As soon as possible after approving the project charter

    C. As soon as possible after completing the RACI chart

    D. As soon as possible after completing the risk register

☑ **B.** As soon as the project charter is complete, the process of identifying project stakeholders should begin.

☒ **A**, **C**, and **D** are incorrect. The project plan includes the initial stakeholder list, and the stakeholder list is needed to create the RACI chart and the risk register.

27. Which project document is initiated and updated with details on project participants, including their expectations?

    A. Requirements documentation

    B. Stakeholder register

    C. Risk register

    D. Project team assignments

    ☑ **B.** Significant changes in the organization or wider stakeholder community would lead the project manager to update the project stakeholder documents such as the engagement plan and the stakeholder register.

    ☒ **A**, **C**, and **D** are incorrect. Re-planning the project is too extreme an action relative to a change in stakeholders for the typical project, and creating new stakeholder documents is unnecessary if they already exist and can be updated. The project charter is not updated after the Initiating process completes.

About the Online Content

This book comes complete with TotalTester Online customizable practice exam software with 600 practice exam questions.

System Requirements

The current and previous major versions of the following desktop browsers are recommended and supported: Chrome, Microsoft Edge, Firefox, and Safari. These browsers update frequently and sometimes an update may cause compatibility issues with the TotalTester Online or other content hosted on the Training Hub. If you run into a problem using one of these browsers, please try using another until the problem is resolved.

Your Total Seminars Training Hub Account

To get access to the online content, you will need to create an account on the Total Seminars Training Hub. Registration is free and you will be able to track all your online content using your account. You may also opt in if you wish to receive marketing information from McGraw-Hill Education or Total Seminars, but this is not required for you to gain access to the online content.

Privacy Notice

McGraw-Hill Education values your privacy. Please be sure to read the Privacy Notice available during registration to see how the information you have provided will be used. You may view our Corporate Customer Privacy Policy by visiting the McGraw-Hill Education Privacy Center. Visit the mheducation.com site and click on "Privacy" at the bottom of the page.

Single User License Terms and Conditions

Online access to the digital content included with this book is governed by the McGraw-Hill Education License Agreement outlined next. By using this digital content, you agree to the terms of that license.

Access   To register and activate your Total Seminars Training Hub account, simply follow these easy steps.

1. Go to **hub.totalsem.com/mheclaim**.

2. To Register and create a new Training Hub account, enter your email address, name, and password. No further information (such as credit card number) is required to create an account.

3. If you already have a Total Seminars Training Hub account, select "Log in" and enter your email and password.

4. Enter your Product Key: `4h6w-kp72-74dh`

5. Click to accept the user license terms.

6. Click "Register and Claim" to create your account. You will be taken to the Training Hub and have access to the content for this book.

Duration of License   Access to your online content through the Total Seminars Training Hub will expire one year from the date the publisher declares the book out of print.

Your purchase of this McGraw-Hill Education product, including its access code, through a retail store is subject to the refund policy of that store.

The Content is a copyrighted work of McGraw-Hill Education and McGraw-Hill Education reserves all rights in and to the Content. The Work is © 2019 by McGraw-Hill Education, LLC.

Restrictions on Transfer   The user is receiving only a limited right to use the Content for user's own internal and personal use, dependent on purchase and continued ownership of this book. The user may not reproduce, forward, modify, create derivative works based upon, transmit, distribute, disseminate, sell, publish, or sublicense the Content or in any way commingle the Content with other third-party content, without McGraw-Hill Education's consent.

Limited Warranty   The McGraw-Hill Education Content is provided on an "as is" basis. Neither McGraw-Hill Education nor its licensors make any guarantees or warranties of any kind, either express or implied, including, but not limited to, implied warranties of merchantability or fitness for a particular purpose or use as to any McGraw-Hill Education Content or the information therein or any warranties as to the accuracy, completeness, correctness, or results to be obtained from, accessing or using the McGraw-Hill Education content, or any material referenced in such content or any information entered into licensee's product by users or other persons and/or any material available on or that can be accessed through the licensee's product (including via any hyperlink or otherwise) or as to non-infringement of third-party rights. Any warranties of any kind, whether express or implied, are disclaimed. Any material or data obtained through use of the McGraw-Hill Education content is at your own discretion and risk and user understands that it will be solely responsible for any resulting damage to its computer system or loss of data.

Neither McGraw-Hill Education nor its licensors shall be liable to any subscriber or to any user or anyone else for any inaccuracy, delay, interruption in service, error or omission, regardless of cause, or for any damage resulting therefrom.

In no event will McGraw-Hill Education or its licensors be liable for any indirect, special or consequential damages, including but not limited to, lost time, lost money, lost profits or good will, whether in contract, tort, strict liability or otherwise, and whether or not such damages are foreseen or unforeseen with respect to any use of the McGraw-Hill Education content.

TotalTester Online

TotalTester Online provides you with a simulation of the CAPM exam. Exams can be taken in Practice Mode or Exam Mode. Practice Mode provides an assistance window with references to the book, explanations of the correct and incorrect answers, and the option to check your answer as you take the test. Exam Mode provides a simulation of the actual exam. The number of questions, the types of questions, and the time allowed are intended to be an accurate representation of the exam environment. The option to customize your quiz allows you to create custom exams from selected domains or chapters, and you can further customize the number of questions and time allowed.

To take a test, follow the instructions provided in the previous section to register and activate your Total Seminars Training Hub account. When you register, you will be taken to the Total Seminars Training Hub. From the Training Hub Home page, select CAPM Practice Exams from the "Study" dropdown menu at the top of the page, or from the list of "Your Topics" on the Home page. Select TotalTester from the menu on the right side of the screen, and then click the icon to load the tester as instructed on the screen. You can then select the option to customize your quiz and begin testing yourself in Practice Mode or Exam Mode. All exams provide an overall grade and a grade broken down by domain.

Technical Support

For questions regarding the TotalTester software or operation of the Training Hub, visit **www .totalsem.com** or e-mail **support@totalsem.com**.

For questions regarding book content, e-mail **hep_customer-service@mheducation.com**. For customers outside the United States, e-mail **international_cs@mheducation.com**.

The CAPM exam is based specifically on the *PMBOK Guide*. The *PMBOK Guide* ensures language and terminology consistency, and it helps ensure that exam questions are rooted in the profession's common, best practices. Take some time to study this glossary to foster an understanding of terms you will see on the CAPM exam.

Acceptance criteria   A set of conditions that must be met before deliverables are accepted by the stakeholders. (Chapter 5)

Actual cost   Realized cost incurred for work performed during a specific time period. (Chapter 7)

Adaptive approaches   Project deliverables are defined iteratively within a project (e.g., agile). (Chapter 5)

Agreements   A contract is a mutually binding agreement that obligates the seller to provide the specified products, services, or results. (Chapter 12)

Assignment matrix   A grid that shows team resources assigned to work packages. (Chapter 9)

Assumption log   The assumption log is a high-level document, and operational assumptions and constraints are normally identified in the business case before the project is initiated and will flow into the project charter. Lower-level activity and task assumptions are generated throughout the project. (Chapter 4)

Backlog   In an agile approach, the backlog is the set of requirements to be implemented in the project. (Chapter 5)

Beta distribution   Cost estimates based on three points as variables into the formula. (Chapter 7)

$$cE = (cO + 4cM + cP) / 6$$

Business requirements   High-level needs of the organization. (Chapter 5)

Close Project or Phase   The process of finalizing all activities for the project, phase, or contract. (Chapter 5)

Colocation   Placing many or all of the most active project team members in the same physical location. (Chapter 9)

Communication skills   The soft skills or people skills needed to manage people doing project work. The top 2 percent of project managers exhibit superior relationship and communication skills. (Chapter 3)

Communications management plan   The communications management plan is a component of the project management plan that describes how project communications will be planned, structured, monitored, and controlled. (Chapter 10)

Conduct Procurements The process of obtaining seller responses, selecting a seller, and awarding a contract. (Chapter 12)

Conflict management Managing conflicts in a timely and constructive way to achieve a high-performing team using five general techniques: withdraw/avoid, smooth/accommodate, compromise/reconcile, force/direct, collaborate/problem-solve. (Chapter 9)

Control Procurements The process of managing procurement relationships, monitoring contract performance and making changes and corrections as appropriate, and closing out contracts. (Chapter 12)

Control Quality The process of monitoring and recording results of executing the quality management activities to assess performance and ensure the project outputs are complete, correct, and meet customer expectations. (Chapter 8)

Control Schedule The process of monitoring the status of the project to update the project schedule and managing changes to the schedule baseline. (Chapter 6)

Control thresholds Targets to compare against cost performance measurements; typically expressed as percentage deviations from the baseline plan. (Chapters 6 and 7)

Cost aggregation Creating a summary of cost estimates by averaging WBS work packages up to control accounts and the entire project. (Chapter 7)

Cost baseline The approved version of the time-phased project budget excluding any management reserves. (Chapter 7)

Cost estimate A quantitative assessment of the likely costs for resources required to complete a given activity; typically expressed in currency (e.g., USD). (Chapter 7)

Cost management plan A component of the project management plan that describes how project costs will be planned, structured, and controlled. (Chapter 7)

Cost performance index (CPI) Ratio of earned value to actual cost to measure efficiency of budgeted resources. (Chapter 7)

$$CPI = EV / AC$$

Cost variance (SV) The delta between the earned value and the actual costs. (Chapter 7)

$$CV = EV - AC$$

Define Activities The process of identifying and documenting the specific actions to be performed to produce the project deliverables. (Chapter 6)

Deliverables Any unique and verifiable product, result, or capability to perform a service that is required to be produced to complete a process, phase, or project. (Chapter 5)

Develop Project Charter The process of developing a document that formally authorizes the existence of a project and provides the project manager with the authority to apply organizational resources to project activities. (Chapter 4)

Develop Project Management Plan   The process of defining, preparing, and coordinating all plan components and consolidating them into an integrated project management plan. (Chapter 4)

Develop Schedule   The process of analyzing activity sequences, durations, resource requirements, and schedule constraints to create a schedule model for project execution and monitoring and controlling. (Chapter 6)

Direct and Manage Project Work   The process of leading and performing the work defined in the project management plan and implementing approved changes to achieve the project's objectives. (Chapter 4)

Directions of influence   Classifies stakeholders based on their influence on the work of the project or the project team in one of four ways: upward, downward, outward, and sideward. (Chapter 12)

Duration   Number of work periods required to complete an activity or WBS component (e.g., hours, days, weeks). (Chapter 7)

Earned value (EV)   The budget associated with authorized work that has been completed. (Chapter 7)

Earned value analysis (EVA)   Compares the performance measurement baseline to the actual schedule and cost performance. (Chapter 7)

Earned value management (EVM)   A methodology to assess project performance and progress by looking at scope, schedule, and resource measurements. (Chapter 7)

Effort   Number of labor units required to complete an activity or WBS component (e.g., hours, days, weeks). (Chapter 7)

Emotional intelligence (EI)   The ability to identify, assess, and manage your own emotions and the emotions of others; useful in reducing tension and increasing cooperation. (Chapter 9)

Estimate Activity Durations   The process of estimating the number of work periods needed to complete individual activities with estimated resources. (Chapter 6)

Event-based risks   Risks that are uncertain future events that must be identified and managed. (Chapter 11)

Hierarchical charts   Charts that show relationships in a graphical, top-down format, including work breakdown structures, organizational breakdown structures, and resource breakdown structures. (Chapter 9)

Impact/influence grid   A 2 × 2 matrix data representation technique used to categorize project stakeholders to assist the team in building positive relationships. Groups stakeholders according to their level of impact on the project versus their influence over the project's outcomes. (Chapter 12)

Influence   The soft skills or people skills needed to have an effect that may change the character, development, or behavior within a project environment. (Chapter 12)

Influencing   Addressing important issues and reaching agreements while maintaining mutual trust. (Chapter 9)

Joint application design/development (JAD)   JADs are facilitated sessions that focus on hosting business subject matter experts (SMEs) and implementation SMEs to quickly develop requirements. (Chapter 5)

Leadership   The ability to lead a team and inspire them to do their jobs well. (Chapter 9)

Level of accuracy   The acceptable range identified by stakeholders for cost estimates (e.g., +/−10%). (Chapter 7)

Level of precision   The rounding to be applied to cost estimates (e.g., USD 595.95 to USD 596 or USD 600). (Chapter 7)

Manage Communications   The process of ensuring timely and appropriate collection, creation, distribution, storage, retrieval, management, monitoring, and ultimate disposition of project information. (Chapter 10)

Manage Project Knowledge   The process of using existing knowledge and creating new knowledge to achieve the project's objectives and contribute to organizational learning. (Chapter 4)

Manage Quality   The process of translating the quality management plan into executable quality activities that incorporate the organization's quality policies into the project. (Chapter 8)

Management reserves   An amount added to the cost baseline to produce the project budget; the change control process is used to access the management reserves during a project. (Chapter 7)

Monitor and Control Project Work   The process of tracking, reviewing, and reporting the overall progress to meet the performance objectives defined in the project management plan. (Chapter 4)

Monitor Communications   The process of ensuring the information needs of the project and its stakeholders are met. (Chapter 10)

Motivation   Providing a reason for someone to act. (Chapter 9)

Nonevent risks   Variability risk and ambiguity risk. (Chapter 11)

Opportunities   Positive risks. (Chapter 11)

Organizational theory   Information regarding the way people, teams, and organizational units behave. (Chapter 9)

Overall project risk strategies   Five alternative strategies: avoid, exploit, transfer/share, mitigate/enhance, or accept. (Chapter 11)

Perform Integrated Change Control   The process of reviewing all change requests; approving changes and managing changes to deliverables, project documents, and the project management plan; and communicating the decisions. (Chapter 4)

Physical resource management Allocating and using physical resources in a project (e.g., material, equipment, supplies). (Chapter 9)

Plan Communications Management The process of developing an appropriate approach and plan for project communications activities based on the information needs of each stakeholder or group, available organizational assets, and the needs of the project. (Chapter 10)

Plan Procurement Management The process of documenting project procurement decisions, specifying the approach, and identifying potential sellers. (Chapter 12)

Plan Quality Management The process of identifying quality requirements and/or standards for the project and its deliverables and documenting how the project will demonstrate compliance with quality requirements and/or standards. (Chapter 8)

Plan Schedule Management The process of establishing the policies, procedures, and documentation for planning, developing, managing, executing, and controlling the project schedule. (Chapter 6)

Planned value (PV) Authorized budget assigned to scheduled work. (Chapter 7)

Power/influence grid A 2 × 2 matrix data representation technique used to categorize project stakeholders to assist the team in building positive relationships. Groups stakeholders according to their level of authority or power in the project versus their influence over the project's outcome. (Chapter 12)

Power/interest grid A 2 × 2 matrix data representation technique used to categorize project stakeholders to assist the team in building positive relationships. Groups stakeholders according to their level of authority or power versus their interest in the project's outcome. (Chapter 12)

Predictive approaches Project deliverables are defined at the beginning of the project (e.g., waterfall). (Chapter 5)

Prioritization In large projects or large communities of stakeholders, it may be necessary to prioritize stakeholder needs. (Chapter 12)

Procurement Management Plan The procurement management plan is a component of the project management plan that describes how a project team will acquire goods and services from outside the performing organization. It describes how the procurement processes will be managed from developing procurement documents through contract closure. A procurement management plan can be formal or informal, can be highly detailed or broadly framed, and is based upon the needs of each project. (Chapter 12)

Product scope The features and functions that characterize a product, service, or result created within a project. (Chapter 5)

Project charter The project charter is the document issued by the project initiator or sponsor that formally authorizes the existence of a project and provides the project manager with the authority to apply organizational resources to project activities. It documents the high-level information on the project and on the product, service, or result the project is intended to satisfy. (Chapter 4)

Project Communications Management In the Project Communications Management knowledge area, project managers focus on making sure that stakeholders are understood in terms of their communications needs. It also involves determining what communication outputs will be exchanged over the course of the project (i.e., status updates, minutes of meetings, reports on deliverables, etc.). (Chapter 10)

Project Integration Management Project Integration Management is a collection of processes required to ensure that the various elements of the projects are properly coordinated. It involves making trade-offs among competing objectives and alternatives to meet or exceed stakeholder needs and expectations. (Chapter 4)

Project management plan The project management plan is a formal approved document that defines the plan for how the project will be executed, monitored, and controlled. (Chapter 4)

Project Procurement Management Project Procurement Management is about establishing, maintaining, and closing relationships with suppliers of goods and services for the project. (Chapter 12)

Project Quality Management Project Quality Management contains the knowledge and processes required to ensure the highest-quality products and deliverables are produced by the project. (Chapter 8)

Project requirements Actions, processes, or other conditions that a project needs to meet. (Chapter 5)

Project resilience Having an empowered project team with budgets and processes in place to cope with emergent risks based on frequent reviews and clear input from stakeholders. (Chapter 11)

Project Schedule Management Project Schedule Management includes the processes required to manage the timely completion of the project. (Chapter 6)

Project scope The work performed to create a product, service, or result within a project. Project scope can include product scope; however, product scope cannot include project scope. (Chapter 5)

Prompt lists A predetermined list of risk categories that might help identify individual project risks and could also act as a source of overall project risk. (Chapter 11)

Qualitative risk analysis An analysis that assesses the relative priority of identified individual project risks using their probability of occurrence. (Chapter 11)

Quality function deployment (QFD) QFD is a facilitation technique using the voice-of-the-customer technique. (Chapter 5)

Quality management plan The quality management plan is a component of the project management plan that describes how the organization's quality policies will be implemented. It describes how the project management team plans to meet the quality requirements set for the project. (Chapter 8)

Quality reports   The quality reports can be graphical, numerical, or qualitative. The information provided can be used by other processes and departments to take corrective actions to achieve the project quality expectations. The information presented in the quality reports may include all quality management issues escalated by the team; recommendations for process, project, and product improvements; corrective actions recommendation (including rework, defect/bugs repair 100 percent inspection, and more); and the summary of findings from the Control Quality process. (Chapter 8)

Quality requirements   Requirements that capture a condition or criteria needed to validate the successful completion of a project deliverable or fulfillment of other project requirements. (Chapter 5)

Quantitative risk analysis   An analysis that assesses quantitative impact of significant risks previously identified in the qualitative risk analysis. (Chapter 11)

RACI   A chart that shows assignments of roles and responsibilities, specifically, Responsible, Accountable, Consulted, and Informed. (Chapter 9)

Requirement   A requirement is a condition or capability that is required to be present in a product, service, or result to satisfy an agreement or other formally imposed specification. (Chapter 5)

Requirements traceability matrix   A grid that links product requirements from their origin to the deliverables that satisfy them. (Chapter 5)

Reserve analysis   Analyzes the status of contingency and management reserves. (Chapter 7)

Resource breakdown structure   A hierarchical representation of resources by category and type; used to acquire and monitor resources. (Chapter 9)

Resource calendar   A calendar that identifies the availability of resources for working days, shifts, start and end of normal business hours, weekends, and public holidays. (Chapter 9)

Resource management plan   A project document that defines the approach to identify different resources needed for the project. (Chapter 9)

Resource planning   Ensuring that enough resources are available for successful project completion. (Chapter 9)

Resource requirements   Requirements that identify the types and quantities of resources required for each work package or activity. (Chapter 9)

Responsiblity assignment matrix (RAM)   A grid that shows team resources assigned to work packages; a RACI chart is an example of a RAM. (Chapter 9)

Risk   An uncertain event or condition that, if realized, can have a positive or negative effect on a project. (Chapter 11)

Risk acceptance   Project team acknowledges the risk and takes action only if it occurs. (Chapter 11)

Risk appetite   The degree of uncertainty an organization or individual is willing to accept in anticipation of a reward. (Chapter 11)

Risk audit   An official inspection used to assess the effectiveness of the risk management process. (Chapter 11)

Risk avoidance   Project team takes steps to eliminate the risk. (Chapter 11)

Risk breakdown structure   A hierarchical representation of potential sources of project risk, including technical risk, management risk, commercial risk, and external risk. (Chapter 11)

Risk data quality assessment   A technique to evaluate the degree to which the data about risks is useful for risk management. (Chapter 11)

Risk enhancement   Project team acknowledges the risk and takes action to increase the probability of occurrence or impact of an opportunity. (Chapter 11)

Risk escalation   Project team acknowledges that a risk is outside its sphere of influence and shifts ownership to a higher level in the organization. (Chapter 11)

Risk exploiting   Project team acknowledges the risk and takes action to ensure that an opportunity occurs. (Chapter 11)

Risk exposure   A quantified loss potential of a risk calculated by multiplying the probability of an incident occurring by its potential financial losses. (Chapter 11)

Risk management plan   A component of the project management plan that describes how risk management activities will be structured and performed. (Chapter 11)

Risk mitigation   Project team acts to decrease the probability of occurrence or impact of a threat. (Chapter 11)

Risk opportunity strategies   Five alternative strategies: escalate, exploit, share, enhance, or accept. (Chapter 11)

Risk owner   Person responsible for monitoring the risks and choosing and implementing an appropriate risk response strategy. (Chapter 11)

Risk register   A component that captures details of individual project risks, including a list of identified risks, potential risk owners, and potential risk responses. (Chapter 11)

Risk report   A report that describes the overall project risk and the current overall project risk status. (Chapter 11)

Risk review   A meeting that examines and documents the effectiveness of risk responses. (Chapter 11)

Risk sharing   Project team allocates ownership of an opportunity to a third party who is best able to capture the benefit of the opportunity. (Chapter 11)

Risk threat strategies   Five alternative strategies: escalate, avoid, transfer, mitigate, or accept. (Chapter 11)

Risk threshold   Level of risk exposure above which risks are addressed and below which risks may be accepted. (Chapter 11)

Risk transference   Project team shifts the impact of a threat to a third party together with ownership of the response. (Chapter 11)

Rules of performance measurement   The decision on how to measure performance in a project (e.g., EVM, WBS control accounts, bottom-up EAC). (Chapter 7)

Salience model   Analyzes stakeholders based on their power (level of authority), urgency, and legitimacy (or proximity). Used for large, complex stakeholder communities to determine relative importance of stakeholders. (Chapter 13)

Schedule baseline   A schedule baseline is the approved version of a schedule model that can be changed only through formal change control procedures and is used as a basis for comparison to actual results. It is accepted and approved by the appropriate stakeholders with baseline start dates and finish dates. During Monitoring and Controlling, the approved baseline dates are compared to the actual start and finish dates to determine whether variances have occurred. The schedule baseline is a component of the project management plan. (Chapter 6)

Schedule management plan   A component of the project management plan that establishes the criteria and the activities for developing, monitoring, and controlling the schedule. The schedule management plan may be formal or informal, highly detailed or broadly framed, based upon the needs of the project, and includes appropriate control thresholds. (Chapter 6)

Scope baseline   The approved version of a scope statement, WBS, and its associated WBS dictionary. (Chapter 5)

Self-organizing teams   Teams that carry out their work without having a centralized point of control; an agile concept. (Chapter 9)

Sequence Activities   The process of identifying and documenting relationships among the project activities. (Chapter 6)

Solution requirements   Requirements that describe the features, functionality, and characteristics of the product, service, or result. (Chapter 5)

Stakeholder   An individual, group, or organization that may affect or be affected by project work, including decisions, activities, and outcome or deliverables. This applies to a project, program, and portfolio. (Chapter 12)

Stakeholder analysis   A systematic technique used to understand the "stake" a stakeholder has in a project, program, and portfolio. Can include noting their interest, rights, ownership, knowledge, and contribution. (Chapter 12)

Stakeholder cube   A three-dimensional representation of the information contained in the three stakeholder analysis grids (power/interest, power/influence, impact/influence). (Chapter 12)

Stakeholder diversity   Identifying how many stakeholders are involved and their cultural backgrounds. This is a consideration for tailoring the approach to stakeholder management. (Chapter 12)

Stakeholder engagement   The measurable involvement of a stakeholder in a project, program, or portfolio. (Chapter 12)

Stakeholder engagement assessment matrix   A point-in-time matrix that compares the current engagement level of a stakeholder group to the desired engagement level of that stakeholder group. Stakeholder engagement levels are listed as one of five levels: unaware, resistant, neutral, supportive, or leading. (Chapter 12)

Stakeholder engagement plan   A plan that identifies strategies and actions to engage stakeholders on a given project, program, or portfolio. Part of the project management plan. (Chapter 12)

Stakeholder register   A project document that catalogs all stakeholders and information about the stakeholders so that project team members can understand what information the stakeholder groups can provide. May also capture expectations of the stakeholders. (Chapter 12)

Stakeholder requirements   Requirements that describe the needs of a stakeholder group. (Chapter 5)

Stakeholder satisfaction   One of the aspects used to measure project success. (Chapter 12)

SWOT analysis   A technique that examines a project from each of the strengths, weaknesses, opportunities, and threats perspectives. (Chapter 11)

Team building   Activities that enhance the team's social relations in order to build a collaborative, cooperative working environment. (Chapter 9)

Team charter   A document that reflects agreed-upon operating guidelines for the team. (Chapter 9)

Threats   Negative risks. (Chapter 11)

To-complete performance index   Ratio that measures the cost performance required to be achieved with the remaining resources in order to meet a specified management goal. (Chapter 7)

$$\text{TCPI} = (BAC - EV) / (BAC - AC) \text{ or } \text{TCPI} = (BAC - EV) / (EAC - AC)$$

Transition requirements   One-time-use-only functionality needed to help move from the current situation to future situations—for example, migrating data from one database to another database. (Chapter 5)

Trend analysis   A data analysis technique that examines project performance over time to determine if performance is improving or deteriorating. (Chapter 5)

Triangular distribution   Cost estimates based on three points as variables into the formula. (Chapter 7)

$$cE = (cO + cM + cP) / 3$$

Tuckman ladder   Five stages of development a team may go through: forming, storming, norming, performing, and adjourning. (Chapter 9)

Units of measure   The dimension used to measure resources (e.g., staff hours, staff days, staff weeks) or quantities used, such as meters, liters, tons, kilometers, or cubic yards. (Chapter 7)

User stories   User stories are short, text-based descriptions of functionality required by a stakeholder group. (Chapter 5)

Variance analysis   A data analysis technique used to compare a baseline to the actual results and determine if the variance (difference) is within the threshold amount or if corrective or preventive action is appropriate. (Chapter 5)

WBS dictionary   A document that provides detailed deliverable, activity, and scheduling information about each component in the WBS. (Chapter 5)

Work breakdown structure (WBS)   The planned work to take place in a project hierarchically decomposed into work packages of 80 hours or less. (Chapter 5)

Work package   The lowest level of the WBS; it is assigned a unique identifier. (Chapter 5)

Single User License Terms and Conditions

Online access to the digital content included with this book is governed by the McGraw-Hill Education License Agreement outlined next. By using this digital content you agree to the terms of that license.

Access   To register and activate your Total Seminars Training Hub account, simply follow these easy steps.

1. Go to **hub.totalsem.com/mheclaim**.
2. To Register and create a new Training Hub account, enter your email address, name, and password. No further information (such as credit card number) is required to create an account.
3. If you already have a Total Seminars Training Hub account, select "Log in" and enter your email and password.
4. Enter your Product Key: **4h6w-kp72-74dh**
5. Click to accept the user license terms.
6. Click "Register and Claim" to create your account. You will be taken to the Training Hub and have access to the content for this book.

Duration of License   Access to your online content through the Total Seminars Training Hub will expire one year from the date the publisher declares the book out of print.

Your purchase of this McGraw-Hill Education product, including its access code, through a retail store is subject to the refund policy of that store.

The Content is a copyrighted work of McGraw-Hill Education and McGraw-Hill Education reserves all rights in and to the Content. The Work is © 2019 by McGraw-Hill Education, LLC.

Restrictions on Transfer   The user is receiving only a limited right to use the Content for user's own internal and personal use, dependent on purchase and continued ownership of this book. The user may not reproduce, forward, modify, create derivative works based upon, transmit, distribute, disseminate, sell, publish, or sublicense the Content or in any way commingle the Content with other third-party content, without McGraw-Hill Education's consent.

Limited Warranty   The McGraw-Hill Education Content is provided on an "as is" basis. Neither McGraw-Hill Education nor its licensors make any guarantees or warranties of any kind, either express or implied, including, but not limited to, implied warranties of merchantability or fitness for a particular purpose or use as to any McGraw-Hill Education Content or the information therein or any warranties as to the accuracy, completeness, currentness, or results to be obtained from, accessing or using the McGraw-Hill Education content, or any material referenced in such content or any information entered into licensee's product by users or other persons and/or any material available on or that can be accessed through the licensee's product (including via any hyperlink or otherwise) or as to non-infringement of third-party rights. Any warranties of any kind, whether express or implied, are disclaimed. Any material or data obtained through use of the McGraw-Hill Education content is at your own discretion and risk and user understands that it will be solely responsible for any resulting damage to its computer system or loss of data.

Neither McGraw-Hill Education nor its licensors shall be liable to any subscriber or to any user or anyone else for any inaccuracy, delay, interruption in service, error or omission, regardless of cause, or for any damage resulting therefrom.

In no event will McGraw-Hill Education or its licensors be liable for any indirect, special or consequential damages, including but not limited to, lost time, lost money, lost profits or good will, whether in contract, tort, strict liability or otherwise, and whether or not such damages are foreseen or unforeseen with respect to any use of the McGraw-Hill Education content.

CPSIA information can be obtained
at www.ICGtesting.com
Printed in the USA
JSHW052326161221
21253JS00004B/27